THE CASE OF T.
EXPLC

"Lon Fuller's Case of the Speluncean Explorers" first appeared in the *Harvard Law Review* in 1949. It is the greatest fictitious legal case of all time. *The Case of the Speluncean Explorers: Nine new opinions* is, however, the first book-length treatment of this classic article available. Peter Suber brings Lon Fuller's portrait of American legal thought up-to-date with contemporary issues in his nine new opinions.

The original case, reprinted here in full, considers five cave explorers who, trapped inside a cave, end up eating one of their companions in order to survive. When they are rescued they are prosecuted for murder, a crime carrying a mandatory death sentence. The legal dilemmas raised by this case were originally addressed by Fuller's five fictitious Supreme Court Justices. Their opinions mirrored the range of legal philosophies dominant in Anglo-American thought half a century ago. Peter Suber has written nine new opinions which reflect changing times, but illuminate the original questions. One of the reasons why this case is so widely cited is that the questions it raises are clearly still pertinent: Are judicial opinions merely rationalizations of the judge's politics and personality? Why do judges disagree so deeply about how the law applies to a particular case? Suber's nine new opinions extend the argument.

Teaching the major positions in jurisprudence painlessly by connecting them to a fascinating and concrete case, this book presupposes no familiarity with law or the philosophy of law. Peter Suber's playful and simple style makes this book an invaluable tool for anyone wanting an introduction to contemporary legal thought.

Peter Suber, who holds a Ph.D. in philosophy and a J.D. (in law), is Professor of Philosophy at Earlham College. He is the author of *The Paradox of Self-Amendment*, the first book-length study of self-reference problems in law.

THE CASE OF THE SPELUNCEAN EXPLORERS

Nine new opinions

Peter Suber

Routledge
Taylor & Francis Group

LONDON AND NEW YORK

First published 1998
by Routledge
2 Park Square, Milton Park, Abingdon, Oxon OX14 4RN

Simultaneously published in the USA and Canada
by Routledge
711 Third Avenue, New York NY 10017

Routledge is an imprint of the Taylor & Francis Group, an informa business

© 1998 Peter Suber

Part I reprinted by kind permission of
The Trustees of the Lon L. Fuller Trust.

Typeset in Baskerville by Routledge
Printed and bound in Great Britain by TJ International Ltd, Padstow, Cornwall

British Library Cataloguing in Publication Data
A catalogue record for this book is available from the British Library

Library of Congress Cataloging in Publication Data
Suber, Peter
The case of the speluncean explorers : nine new opinions / Peter Suber
p :cm.
Includes bibliographical references and index.
1. Law—Philosophy. 2. Fuller, Lon L., 1902- —Contributions in law. I. Title.
K230.F842S8 1998
340'.1—dc21

ISBN 10: 0-415-18546-7 (pbk)
ISBN 10: 0-415-18545-9 (hbk)

ISBN 13: 978-0-415-18546-2 (pbk)
ISBN 13: 978-0-415-18545-5 (hbk)

FOR MY MOTHER,
GRACE MAY STERN,
PROBISSIMAE LEGUM SCRIPTORI.
NON ERAT UNA PUERORUM.

CONTENTS

CONTENTS

PREFACE

Lon Fuller's *Case of the Speluncean Explorers* is the greatest fictitious legal case of all time. That is saying a lot, for it has some stiff competition. While its competitors may outdo it in courtroom drama, character development, or investigative suspense, none matches it in legal depth or dialectical agility. It shows not what makes some lawyer's caseload interesting, but what makes law itself interesting. It would not make a good movie; it is all "talking heads." In fact, the parts that *would* make a good movie – the events within the cave – are over and done with by the time Fuller begins his piece. Moreover, these events are not depicted with cinematic vivacity, but described after the fact with judicial precision and blandness.

Fuller's five Supreme Court justices tranquilly but rigorously show the complexity of the facts and the flexibility of legal reasoning. The five opinions focus on different factual details and legal precedents, and fit them into different background structures of legal and political principle. By these means Fuller crystallizes important conflicts of principle and illustrates the major schools of legal philosophy in his day. Fuller's case has been called "a classic in jurisprudence," "a microcosm of this century's debates," and a "breathtaking intellectual accomplishment."*

Although only half a century separates us from the date of Fuller's essay, the legal landscape has changed profoundly. I have written nine new judicial opinions on his case, with roughly Fuller's own objectives in view, hoping to explore important issues of principle and in the process to bring the depiction of legal philosophy up to date.

While I would like to depict the major schools of legal philosophy today, giving each its due, there are a few obstacles that subtly constrain the project.

---

* The first quotation is from Anthony D'Amato, "The Speluncean Explorers – Further Proceedings," *Stanford Law Review*, 1980, vol. 32, pp. 467–85 at p. 467. The second and third are from William N. Eskridge, Jr, "The Case of the Speluncean Explorers: Twentieth-Century Statutory Interpretation in a Nutshell," *George Washington Law Review*, August 1993, vol. 61, no. 6, pp. 1731–53 at p. 1732.

First, I must stick to the facts and law of this case. I cannot illustrate a contemporary legal philosophy using its own favorite examples, but must discover how it would approach the case of the speluncean explorers. Fortunately most of the major contemporary movements in jurisprudence can find a foothold in these facts, which we may take as one small symptom of their depth and generality.

Second, I would like to say something new about the case. Before I began to write these opinions, I unreflectively assumed that Fuller's five justices had already offered just about every plausible legal argument that could be brought to bear on these facts. But once I gave myself the assignment, some resolute, quasi-speluncean exploration persuaded me that I had been mistaken. Now I have nearly the opposite conviction: to say that serious thinking about this case has been exhausted is to say that serious thinking about law, adjudication, crime, homicide, punishment, excuse, justification, and justice have been exhausted.

Third, I cannot have more than nine opinions. More would begin to strain credibility and tire even the generous reader of good will. The bad news is that there are far more than nine important movements and strands of contemporary legal thought. The good news is that they are not all incompatible. I could not embody every distinct strand of contemporary thought in a distinct opinion; and I did not want to limit myself to just nine positions. So I have blended perspectives when consistency and plausibility allowed. This meant, in turn, that the purity of individual opinions could not be a constraint.

Finally, I felt the same tug that Fuller must have felt to arrange for a tie vote – the tug of pedagogical neutrality, requiring that I place the burden of decision squarely on the reader. The odd number of judges is only one obstacle here. Some movements in contemporary jurisprudence naturally pull toward acquittal, and some toward conviction. If I find more of one kind than another, then I must combine some of the "majority" opinions, or multiply some of the "minority" views, or dig more deeply for other veins of contemporary thought.

At times I also felt constrained not to invent new facts about the history of Newgarth, and to play within the four corners of the playground I inherited from Fuller. But at other times I felt that to play this game in Lon Fuller's spirit I was entitled to a few liberties. I have kept my own inventions to a minimum, hoping they would not be material to the holding. At some points I found that I was required to take the paths of "restraint" and "activism" at the same time. For example, I resolved to invent no new legal precedents for Newgarth, and nearly succeeded, but that forced me to invent an explanation for the small number of cases cited by the Court.

The result of all these constraints is that some contemporary movements are not represented, some are blended as far as consistency allows with others, and some are given undue prominence by their recalcitrance to be so blended. What emerges is one person's updating of Lon Fuller's group portrait of American legal philosophies and a deeper exploration of the issues raised by his case.

It follows from these constraints that there is not a one-to-one correspondence between these opinions and nine schools of contemporary jurisprudence. Both ways of deviating from one-to-one correspondence are present here. Blending sometimes put more than one contemporary movement into one opinion, and disagreements within a movement over details or direction sometimes required that it be represented in more than one opinion.

Each opinion has a dominant orientation within jurisprudence, but each also shows the mixed doctrinal influences and variations on the theme that real opinions do. Or at least I hope the opinions show this much real texture, for my constraints did not force all of it.

At the end of his article (p. 32, below), Fuller wrote, "The reader . . . who seeks to trace out contemporary resemblances where none is intended or contemplated, should be warned that he is engaged in a frolic of his own, which may possibly lead him to miss whatever modest truths are contained in the opinions delivered by the Supreme Court of Newgarth." If the first half of this sentence means that Fuller intended no resemblances, then he must have been winking. But if he meant that there are undoubtedly resemblances he did not intend, and that identifying any of the resemblances is less profitable than confronting the arguments, then I embrace his gentle warning and adopt it as my own.

The second half of Fuller's sentence I adopt with no hedging or winking. The positions I have distilled into judicial opinions are serious and significant attempts to understand the nature of law. Whether they contain only "modest truths" or truths of a grander kind is the primary question here for the student, scholar, and citizen. I wrote for the reader who is less interested in position-labeling and allusion-hunting than in grappling with these serious and significant arguments, assessing their strengths and weaknesses, and seeing how they matter for a concrete case. For these reasons, I hope that scholars who are already familiar with the positions represented here will not put secondary questions ahead of primary ones, except as a frolic of their own. For the same reasons, I do not believe these nine opinions presuppose any acquaintance with contemporary law or philosophy of law.

I am not the first to write new opinions on the *Case of the Speluncean Explorers*. Anthony D'Amato wrote three for the *Stanford Law Review* in 1980 (vol. 32, pp. 467–85), and Naomi Cahn, John Calmore, Mary Coombs, Dwight Greene, Geoffrey Miller, Jeremy Paul, and Laura Stein wrote one apiece, from different legal and political standpoints, for the *George Washington Law Review* in 1993 (vol. 61, pp. 1754–1811). I recommend D'Amato's three opinions for their clear exploration of the moral issues raised by the case. I recommend the George Washington Seven for opinions that are more pure, or less mixed, than mine in their representation of contemporary positions, and more willing to invent new facts about Newgarth in order to permit sharper comment on the state of American law.

When reading Fuller's original piece one naturally asks which of the contending legal philosophies is most acceptable, most compelling, most persuasive. In addition, however, one wonders whether the plurality and incompatibility of these legal philosophies it itself a clue to the nature of adjudication. Is all judicial reasoning just *ex post facto* rationalization of ideology and interest, politics and personality? This question was an important one in Fuller's day and is, if anything, even more important today. The question is raised less by any single opinion than by the spectrum of opinions. Each is reasoned in its own way, but what does this show about reasoning itself? If legal reasoning is infinitely flexible, if it can serve any master, if (as Hume said of reason in general) it is the slave of the passions, then the idea that law constrains judges would be entirely illusory. But if law properly understood does constrain judges, then why do reasonable judges disagree so deeply? I am happy that my project raises these questions, and just as happy that it does not permit me to digress from law into philosophy in order to answer them. That is another project for another time.

I gratefully thank the estate of Lon Fuller for permission to reprint his article in this volume. If I could not include his original text, my book would be impoverished and untethered. I thank Deanna Airgood for her speedy and accurate typing of Fuller's article, and Jennifer Laurin for her sharp proofreading eye. I thank Jim Bower, Marya Bower, Len Clark, Hal Hanes, Pablo Nagel, Mark Packer, Diana Punzo, Vince Punzo, Monteze Snyder, A.L.P. Thorpe, and two reviewers for Routledge, for their helpful comments on an earlier draft of these opinions. I thank A. Varner Seaman for the "body shield" analogy that I gave to Justice Goad. Finally, I thank my philosophy of law students over the past fifteen years for their insights, for their passion, for seeing what was at stake, and for their willingness to let a fictitious legal case teach them something important about law in the real world.

INTRODUCTION

Fuller based his fictitious case on some disturbingly real ones. The two uppermost in his mind were undoubtedly *U.S. v. Holmes* (1842) and *Regina v. Dudley & Stephens* (1884), two lifeboat cases in which disaster at sea was followed by homicide and prosecution. In the *Holmes* case, the homicides were to lighten a badly overloaded lifeboat. In *Dudley & Stephens*, the homicide was to create a meal for the starving survivors.

In *Holmes*, an immigrant ship, the *William Brown*, en route from Liverpool to Philadelphia, hit an iceberg and sank off the coast of Newfoundland. The eighty passengers and crew had to share two lifeboats. Forty-one passengers and sailors ended up in a twenty-two-foot longboat. Nine officers and crew members occupied the smaller jolly boat, built for six or seven. The remaining thirty souls were left to go down with the ship; most were children; not one was crew. The captain ordered a mate, with a map and compass, to join the longboat. This made forty-two in the longboat, eight in the jolly boat. The longboat had oars but no sails; the jolly boat had both.

The jolly boat moved toward the Newfoundland coast where it was eventually picked up by a fishing vessel. The longboat was too overloaded to move and drifted for a day, its gunwales perilously close to the water. As the weather picked up, water began spilling into the boat. Already leaky, the longboat sprang a larger hole that required feverish bailing. After being swamped by a few large waves, it teetered on the verge of going down. The mate shouted to the sailors to lighten the load. Sailor Holmes responded, and with the help of another sailor, tossed more than six men and two women overboard. The next morning he tossed two more men overboard.

They drifted east, fighting starvation with their meager rations, and were picked up off the French coast a few weeks later. Their story fascinated and shocked the world. Those survivors who returned to the United States pressed the Philadelphia district attorney to prosecute the longboat sailors for murder. Unluckily, Holmes was the only sailor from the longboat in Philadelphia at the time, and was arrested. The grand jury would not indict him for murder, forcing the prosecutor to reduce the charge to voluntary manslaughter.

Holmes offered a necessity defense. If the killings were necessary for the

1

survival of those on board, he argued, then they were legally justified. The case was heard by U.S. Supreme Court Justice Henry Baldwin, temporarily sitting as a Philadelphia trial judge. He instructed the jury that some sailors were needed to navigate the longboat; but beyond that critical number, they were not entitled to any privilege over the passengers. The excess sailors must stand their chances in a lottery with the passengers. With these instructions, the jury convicted Holmes of voluntary manslaughter. Justice Baldwin sentenced him six months in prison and fined him twenty dollars. Holmes served his prison time, but was spared the fine when pardoned by President John Tyler.

In the *Dudley & Stephens* case, the sinking of the Australian yacht *Mignonette*, en route from Essex to Sydney, threw four survivors into one thirteen-foot lifeboat, with only two cans of turnips for food. Thomas Dudley was the captain, Edwin Stephens the mate, Edwin Brooks an able seaman, and Richard Parker an ordinary seaman. Parker was seventeen years old and, before long, clearly the most sickly and ailing of the four. The four sailors made one can of turnips last two days, and had nothing but rain water for the two days after that, when they caught a turtle. They finished the second can of turnips the same day, perhaps thinking they could catch another turtle. A week later they had eaten everything edible from the turtle, and there was still no sign of rescue in sight. Nor were they able to catch any other food. Their lips and tongue blackened from dehydration, their feet and legs swollen, and their skin covered in unhealing sores, they began to drink their urine. Parker drank seawater, which sailors believed would bring certain death.

On the nineteenth day Dudley proposed a lottery in which one of them would be killed and eaten by the rest. Brooks said *no* and Stephens was indecisive, so they put the plan aside. Dudley then spoke in confidence to Stephens. Parker would die first anyway, from his weakened condition; and he had no family. Why wait? Stephens was persuaded. Dudley then killed Parker, and all three fed on his body.

They fed on the body for four days, and finished about half of it, before they were rescued by the German sailing ship *Moctezuma*, en route from Punta Arenas, Chile, to Hamburg. When the *Moctezuma* put in at Falmouth on the way home, Dudley, Stephens, and Brooks were arrested for murder and taken into custody.

The decision to prosecute them for murder was approved by Sir William Harcourt, the British home secretary, after consulting with the attorney general, solicitor general, and officers of the crown. But the Falmouth public was entirely on the side of the defendants. Fearing acquittal, the judge asked the jury for a special verdict. This meant that the jury was asked only to find the facts, not to rule on the ultimate question whether the facts amounted to murder. (This procedure allowed the court to convict the defendants even with a sympathetic jury.) On the facts found by the jury, the judge convicted the defendants of murder, rejecting their necessity defense. He sentenced them to hang, but they were pardoned by Queen Victoria, on the advice of the same Sir William Harcourt who had recommended prosecution.

For more information see A.W. Brian Simpson's engrossing and detailed accounts in *Cannibalism and the Common Law* (University of Chicago Press, 1984). The stories are retold more briefly and dramatically in Leo Katz's excellent meditation on the criminal law, *Bad Acts and Guilty Minds* (University of Chicago Press, 1987). Excerpts from the judicial opinions are often found in casebooks used in Anglo-American law schools.

One can easily see the large clusters of fact that Fuller borrowed from these cases for his own: extremities of desperation, lotteries, cannibalism, popular sympathy for the defendants, politically difficult prosecutions, defenses of stark necessity, jury convictions, the possibility of pardons. Even small details, like the jury's special verdict in *Dudley & Stephens*, come up again in Fuller's case. But an inventory of these borrowed elements only brings into relief the extent of Fuller's creativity. He moved the accident from the high seas to a cave within Newgarth. This simultaneously sharpened questions about jurisdiction and permitted the all-important radio communications. He added the radio, and the expert medical and engineering opinions delivered by the radio; these gave the spelunkers reliable knowledge, not mere panic surmise, that starvation would come before rescue. He added the foresight of the spelunkers to ask their professional organization to begin a rescue if they did not return by a certain date. He added the ten workmen killed in the rescue attempt. He added the complex dance of Whetmore's consent: at first consenting to join the death pact, then revoking his consent, then assenting to the fairness of the dice throw made on his behalf by the others. He added the Newgarthian history of social contract and civil war, the mandatory death penalty for murder, the ancient act of judicial legislation that created the exception for self-defense, and dozens of other details, including a handful of precedents, whose weight and significance each judge measures differently.

It would oversimplify Fuller's ingenuity to say that he fine-tuned the facts until the case for acquittal was just about exactly as strong as the case for conviction. For if that were so, then conscientious judges would be unable to make up their minds, or would do so only in great uncertainty, with large concessions to the other side. Instead, Fuller fine-tuned the facts until they gave some kinds of judges good grounds to acquit, and other kinds of judges good grounds to convict. Most judges of both kinds are quite sure that the facts are not balanced, and that the imbalance should be read their way. If in the end there are as many votes to acquit as to convict, this is due less to the balance of the facts than to the balance of legal philosophies on the high court. Good judges are philosophically diverse; Fuller fine-tuned the facts in order to draw attention to this diversity of legal thought.

The case would be balanced in a broader sense if the several opinions were equally strong in their arguments or equally faithful to the law. But it would short-circuit Fuller's shrewdness and hard work to suppose that these diverse legal philosophies were equally adequate just because he includes them in the case, or just because they have arguments to offer, or just because they authentically emerge from important moral, legal, political, or philosophical traditions. This is just what we should think about, not what we should take from the case without thinking; it is not Fuller's conclusion, but his question.

A case whose facts are balanced in this special way, giving judges of different persuasions good grounds to find the facts unbalanced in different directions, is not so peculiar that it cannot teach us anything about real cases. On the contrary, most cases that stir public controversy possess the same troublesome property. For example, consider recent Supreme Court cases asking whether statutes prohibiting sodomy, flag burning, or assisted suicide are constitutional. The public divides on them, as if the facts were balanced, but individual judgments are strongly held, as if the facts were not balanced. Actually, of course, the balance lies less in the facts themselves than in the legal principles and perspectives held by the American public. This is just the complex and delicate sort of balance that Fuller achieved in his case, through his cunning invention of the facts and his judicious reading of the judiciary. That is only one reason why his case can teach us very much indeed about our own hard cases.

Lon Fuller (1902–78) was a Texan, educated at Stanford, who taught at Harvard. The author of eight books* and many articles, he was one of the leading legal philosophers of the 20th century. He conducted a long-running dispute in the law journals with H.L.A. Hart on the merits of positivism in law; Fuller took the anti-positivist position. To his credit, if one did not already know that Fuller was critical of legal positivism, then an honest reading of *The Case of the Speluncean Explorers* would not reveal it. In his major statement of legal philosophy, *The Morality of Law* (1964), he drew together and made systematic his case against positivism and argued for a limited form of natural law. As an appendix, he included his second and less famous, fictitious legal case, *The Case of the Grudge Informer*.

I've heard that Fuller was a superb contracts professor. But he died the year before I entered law school and I have not read his case book on contracts. To me his greatness lies in his lifelong proof that rigorous legal thought does not exclude creativity, does not require jargon, and does not make morality an independent variable or an afterthought.

---

* *Law in Quest of Itself*, Foundation Press, 1940; *Reason and Fiat in Case Law*, American Book-Stratford Press, 1943; *Basic Contract Law*, West Publishing Co., 1947, 2nd edn, 1964; *Problems of Jurisprudence*, Foundation Press, 1949; *Human Purpose and Natural Law*, Notre Dame Law School, 1958; *The Morality of Law*, Yale University Press, 1964, rev. edn, 1969; *Legal Fictions*, Stanford University Press, 1967; and *Anatomy of Law*, Praeger, 1968.

Part I

LON FULLER'S *CASE OF THE SPELUNCEAN EXPLORERS*

In the Supreme Court of Newgarth, 4300 *

The defendants, having been indicted for the crime of murder, were convicted and sentenced to be hanged by the Court of General Instances of the County of Stowfield. They bring a petition of error before this Court. The facts sufficiently appear in the opinion of the Chief Justice.

* The opinions stated in Part I have been reprinted with permission from Lon L. Fuller, "The Case of the Speluncean Explorers," *Harvard Law Review*, 1949, vol. 62, no. 4, pp. 616–45.

OPINION OF CHIEF JUSTICE TRUEPENNY

The four defendants are members of the Speluncean Society, an organization of amateurs interested in the exploration of caves. Early in May of 4299 they, in the company of Roger Whetmore, then also a member of the Society, penetrated into the interior of a limestone cavern of the type found in the Central Plateau of this Commonwealth. While they were in a position remote from the entrance to the cave, a landslide occurred. Heavy boulders fell in such a manner as to block completely the only known opening to the cave. When the men discovered their predicament, they settled themselves near the obstructed entrance to wait until a rescue party should remove the detritus that prevented them from leaving their underground prison. On the failure of Whetmore and the defendants to return to their homes, the Secretary of the Society was notified by their families. It appears that the explorers had left indications at the headquarters of the Society concerning the location of the cave they proposed to visit. A rescue party was promptly dispatched to the spot.

The task of rescue proved one of overwhelming difficulty. It was necessary to supplement the forces of the original party by repeated increments of men and machines, which had to be conveyed at great expense to the remote and isolated region in which the cave was located. A huge temporary camp of workmen, engineers, geologists, and other experts was established. The work of removing the obstruction was several times frustrated by fresh landslides. In one of these, ten of the workmen engaged in clearing the entrance were killed. The treasury of the Speluncean Society was soon exhausted in the rescue effort, and the sum of eight hundred thousand frelars, raised partly by popular subscription and partly by legislative grant, was expended before the imprisoned men were rescued. Success was finally achieved on the thirty-second day after the men entered the cave.

Since it was known that the explorers had carried with them only scant provisions, and since it was also known that there was no animal or vegetable matter within the cave on which they might subsist, anxiety was early felt that they might meet death by starvation before access to them could be obtained. On the twentieth day of their imprisonment it was learned for the first time that they had taken with them into the cave a portable wireless machine capable of both

7

sending and receiving messages. A similar machine was promptly installed in the rescue camp and oral communication established with the unfortunate men within the mountain. They asked to be informed how long a time would be required to release them. The engineers in charge of the project answered that at least ten days would be required even if no new landslides occurred. The explorers then asked if any physicians were present, and were placed in communication with a committee of medical experts. The imprisoned men described their condition and the rations they had taken with them, and asked for a medical opinion whether they would be likely to live without food for ten days longer. The chairman of the committee of physicians told them that there was little possibility of this. The wireless machine within the cave then remained silent for eight hours. When communication was re-established, the men asked to speak again with the physicians. The chairman of the physicians' committee was placed before the apparatus, and Whetmore, speaking on behalf of himself and the defendants, asked whether they would be able to survive for ten days longer if they consumed the flesh of one of their number. The physicians' chairman reluctantly answered this question in the affirmative. Whetmore asked whether it would be advisable for them to cast lots to determine which of them should be eaten. None of the physicians present was willing to answer the question. Whetmore then asked if there were among the party a judge or other official of the government who would answer this question. None of those attached to the rescue camp was willing to assume the role of advisor in this matter. He then asked if any minister or priest would answer their question, and none was found who would do so. Thereafter no further messages were received from within the cave, and it was assumed (erroneously, it later appeared) that the electric batteries of the explorers' wireless machine had become exhausted. When the imprisoned men were finally released, it was learned that on the twenty-third day after their entrance into the cave Whetmore had been killed and eaten by his companions.

From the testimony of the defendants, which was accepted by the jury, it appears that it was Whetmore who first proposed that they might find the nutriment without which survival was impossible in the flesh of one of their own number. It was also Whetmore who first proposed the use of some method of casting lots, calling the attention of the defendants to a pair of dice he happened to have with him. The defendants were at first reluctant to adopt so desperate a procedure, but after the conversations by wireless related above, they finally agreed on the plan proposed by Whetmore. After much discussion of the mathematical problems involved, agreement was finally reached on a method of determining the issue by the use of the dice.

Before the dice were cast, however, Whetmore declared that he withdrew from the arrangement, as he had decided on reflection to wait for another week before embracing an expedient so frightful and odious. The others charged him with a breach of faith and proceeded to cast the dice. When it came Whetmore's turn, the dice were cast for him by one of the defendants, and he was asked to declare any objections he might have to the fairness of the throw. He stated that he had no such objections. The throw went against him, and he was then put to death and eaten by his companions.

After the rescue of the defendants, and after they had completed a stay in a hospital where they underwent a course of treatment for malnutrition and shock, they were indicted for the murder of Roger Whetmore. At the trial, after the testimony had been concluded, the foreman of the jury (a lawyer by profession) inquired of the court whether the jury might not find a special verdict, leaving it to the court to say whether on the facts as found the defendants were guilty. After some discussion, both the Prosecutor and counsel for the defendants indicated their acceptance of this procedure, and it was adopted by the court. In a lengthy special verdict the jury found the facts as I have related them above, and found further that if on these facts the defendants were guilty of the crime charged against them, then they found the defendants guilty. On the basis of this verdict, the trial judge ruled that the defendants were guilty of murdering Roger Whetmore. The judge then sentenced them to be hanged, the law of our Commonwealth permitting him no discretion with respect to the penalty to be imposed. After the release of the jury, its members joined in communication to the Chief Executive asking that the sentence be commuted to an imprisonment of six months. The trial judge addressed a similar communication of the Chief Executive. As yet no action with respect to these pleas has been taken, as the Chief Executive is apparently awaiting our disposition of this petition of error.

It seems to me that in dealing with this extraordinary case the jury and the trial judge followed a course that was not only fair and wise, but the only course that was open to them under the law. The language of our statute is well known: "Whoever shall willfully take the life of another shall be punished by death," N.C.S.A. (N.S.) §12-A. This statute permits of no exception applicable to this case, however, our sympathies may incline us to make allowance for the tragic situation in which these men found themselves.

In a case like this the principle of executive clemency seems admirably suited to mitigate the rigors of the law, and I propose to my colleagues that we follow the example of the jury and the trial judge by joining in the communications they have addressed to the Chief Executive. There is every reason to believe that these requests for clemency will be heeded, coming as they do from those who have studied the case and had an opportunity to become thoroughly acquainted with all its circumstances. It is highly improbable that the Chief Executive would deny these requests unless he were himself to hold hearings at least as extensive as those involved in the trial below, which lasted for three months. The holding of such hearings (which would virtually amount to a retrial of the case) would scarcely be compatible with the function of the Executive as it is usually conceived. I think we may therefore assume that some form of clemency will be extended to these defendants. If this is done, then justice will be accomplished without impairing either the letter or spirit of our statutes and without offering any encouragement for the disregard of law.

OPINION OF JUSTICE FOSTER

I am shocked that the Chief Justice, in an effort to escape the embarrassments of this tragic case, should have adopted, and should have proposed to his colleagues, an expedient at once so sordid and so obvious. I believe something more is on trial in this case than the fate of these unfortunate explorers; that is the law of our Commonwealth. If this Court declares that under our law these men have committed a crime, then our law is itself convicted in the tribunal of common sense, no matter what happens to the individuals involved in this petition of error. For us to assert that the law we uphold and expound compels us to a conclusion we are ashamed of, and from which we can only escape by appealing to a dispensation resting within the personal whim of the Executive, seems to me to amount to an admission that the law of this Commonwealth no longer pretends to incorporate justice.

For myself, I do not believe that our law compels the monstrous conclusion that these men are murderers. I believe, on the contrary, that it declares them to be innocent of any crime. I rest this conclusion on two independent grounds, either of which is of itself sufficient to justify the acquittal of these defendants.

The first of these grounds rests on a premise that may arouse opposition until it has been examined candidly. I take the view that the enacted or positive law of this Commonwealth, including all of its statutes and precedents, is inapplicable to this case, and that the case is governed instead by what ancient writers in Europe and America called "the law of nature."

This conclusion rests on the proposition that our positive law is predicated on the possibility of men's coexistence in society. When a situation arises in which the coexistence of men becomes impossible, then a condition that underlies all of our precedents and statutes has ceased to exist. When that condition disappears, then it is my opinion that the force of our positive law disappears with it. We are not accustomed to applying the maxim *cessante ratione legis, cessat et ipsa lex* [where the reason for the law ceases, the law itself ceases] to the whole of our enacted law, but I believe that this is a case where the maxim should be so applied.

The proposition that all positive law is based on the possibility of men's coexistence has a strange sound, not because the truth it contains is strange, but simply because it is a truth so obvious and pervasive that we seldom have occasion to give words to it. Like the air we breathe, it so pervades our environment that we forget that it exists until we are suddenly deprived of it. Whatever particular objects may be sought by the various branches of our law, it is apparent on reflection that all of them are directed toward facilitating and improving men's coexistence and regulating with fairness and equity the relations of their life in common. When the assumption that men may live together loses its truth, as it obviously did in this extraordinary situation where life only became possible by the taking of life, then the basic premises underlying our whole legal order have lost their meaning and force.

Had the tragic events of this case taken place a mile beyond the territorial limits of our Commonwealth, no one would pretend that our law was applicable to them. We recognize that jurisdiction rests on a territorial basis. The grounds of this principle are by no means obvious and are seldom examined. I take it that this principle is supported by an assumption that it is feasible to impose a single legal order upon a group of men only if they live together within the confines of a given area of the earth's surface. The premise that men shall coexist in a group underlies, then, the territorial principle, as it does all of law. Now I contend that a case may be removed morally from the force of a legal order, as well as geographically. If we look to the purposes of law and government, and to the premises underlying our positive law, these men when they made their fateful decision were as remote from our legal order as if they had been a thousand miles beyond our boundaries. Even in a physical sense, their underground prison was separated from our courts and writ-servers by a solid curtain of rock that could be removed only after the most extraordinary expenditures of time and effort.

I conclude, therefore, that at the time Roger Whetmore's life was ended by these defendants, they were, to use the quaint language of nineteenth-century writers, not in a "state of civil society" but in a "state of nature." This has the consequence that the law applicable to them is not the enacted and established law of this Commonwealth, but the law derived from those principles that were appropriate to their condition. I have no hesitancy in saying that under those principles they were guiltless of any crime.

What these men did was done in pursuance of an agreement accepted by all of them and first proposed by Whetmore himself. Since it was apparent that their extraordinary predicament made inapplicable the usual principles that regulate men's relations with one another, it was necessary for them to draw, as it were, a new charter of government appropriate to the situation in which they found themselves.

It has from antiquity been recognized that the most basic principle of law or government is to be found in the notion of contract or agreement. Ancient thinkers, especially during the period from 1600 to 1900, used to base government itself on a supposed original social compact. Skeptics pointed out that this theory contradicted the known facts of history, and that there was no scientific evidence to support the notion that any government was ever founded in the manner supposed by the theory. Moralists replied that, if the compact was a fiction from a historical point of view, the notion of compact or agreement furnished the only ethical justification on which the powers of government, which include that of taking life, could be rested. The powers of government can only be justified morally on the ground that these are powers that reasonable men would agree upon and accept if they were faced with the necessity of constructing anew some order to make their life in common possible.

Fortunately, our Commonwealth is not bothered by the perplexities that beset the ancients. We know as a matter of historical truth that our government was founded upon a contract or free accord of men. The archeological proof is conclusive that in the first period following the Great Spiral the survivors of that holocaust voluntarily came together and drew up a charter of government. Sophistical writers have raised questions as to the power of those remote contractors to bind future generations, but the fact remains that our government traces itself back in an unbroken line to that original charter.

If, therefore, our hangmen have the power to end men's lives, if our sheriffs have the power to put delinquent tenants in the street, if our police have the power to incarcerate the inebriated reveler, these powers find their moral justification in that original compact of our forefathers. If we can find no higher source for our legal order, what higher source should we expect these starving unfortunates to find for the order they adopted for themselves?

I believe that the line of argument I have just expounded permits of no rational answer. I realize that it will probably be received with a certain discomfort by many who read this opinion, who will be inclined to suspect that some hidden sophistry must underlie a demonstration that leads to so many unfamiliar conclusions. The source of this discomfort is, however, easy to identify. The usual conditions of human existence incline us to think of human life as an absolute value, not to be sacrificed under any circumstances. There is much that is fictitious about this conception even when it is applied to the ordinary relations of society. We have an illustration of this truth in the very case before us. Ten workmen were killed in the process of removing the rocks from the opening to the cave. Did not the engineers and government officials who directed the rescue effort know that the operations they were undertaking were dangerous and involved a serious risk to the lives of the workmen executing them? If it was proper that these ten lives should be sacrificed to save the lives of five imprisoned explorers, why then are we told it was wrong for these explorers to carry out an arrangement which would save four lives at the cost of one?

Every highway, every tunnel, every building we project involves a risk to human life. Taking these projects in the aggregate, we can calculate with some precision how many deaths the construction of them will require; statisticians can tell you the average cost in human lives of a thousand miles of a four-lane concrete highway. Yet we deliberately and knowingly incur and pay this cost on the assumption that the values obtained for those who survive outweigh the loss. If these things can be said of a society functioning above ground in a normal and ordinary manner, what shall we say of the supposed absolute value of a human life in the desperate situation in which these defendants and their companion Whetmore found themselves?

This concludes the exposition of the first ground of my decision. My second ground proceeds by rejecting hypothetically all the premises on which I have so far proceeded. I concede for purposes of argument that I am wrong in saying that the situation of these men removed them from the effect of our positive law, and I assume that the Consolidated Statutes have the power to penetrate 500 feet of rock and to impose themselves upon these starving men huddled in their underground prison.

Now it is, of course, perfectly clear that these men did an act that violates the literal wording of the statute which declares that he who "shall willfully take the life of another" is a murderer. But one of the most ancient bits of legal wisdom is the saying that a man may break the letter of the law without breaking the law itself. Every proposition of positive law, whether contained in a statute or a judicial precedent, is to be interpreted reasonably, in the light of its evident purpose. This is a truth so elementary that it is hardly necessary to expatiate on it. Illustrations of its application are numberless and are to be found in every branch of law. In *Commonwealth v. Staymore* the defendant was convicted under a statute making it a crime to leave one's car parked in certain areas for a period longer than two hours. The defendant had attempted to remove his car, but was prevented from doing so because the streets were obstructed by a political demonstration in which he took no part and which he had no reason to anticipate. His conviction was set aside by this Court, although his case fell squarely within the wording of the statute. Again, in *Fehler v. Neegas* there was before this Court for construction a statute, in which the word "not" had plainly been transposed from its intended position in the final and most crucial section of the act. This transposition was contained in all the successive drafts of the act, where it was apparently overlooked by the draftsmen and sponsors of the legislation. No one was able to prove how the error came about, yet it was apparent that, taking account of the contents of the statute as a whole, an error had been made, since a literal reading of the final clause rendered it inconsistent with everything that had gone before and with the object of the enactment as stated in its preamble. This Court refused to accept a literal interpretation of the statute, and in effect rectified its language by reading the word "not" into the place where it was evidently intended to go.

The statute before us for interpretation has never been applied literally. Centuries ago it was established that a killing in self-defense is excused. There is nothing in the wording of the statute that suggests this exception. Various attempts have been made to reconcile the legal treatment of self-defense with the words of the statute, but in my opinion these are all merely ingenious sophistries. The truth is that the exception in favor of self-defense cannot be reconciled with the *words* of the statute, but only with its *purpose*.

The true reconciliation of the excuse of self-defense with the statute making it

13

a crime to kill another is to be found in the following line of reasoning. One of the principal objects underlying any criminal legislation is that of deterring men from crime. Now it is apparent that if it were declared to be the law that a killing in self-defense is murder such a rule could not operate in a deterrent manner. A man whose life is threatened will repel his aggressor, whatever the law may say. Looking therefore to the broad purposes of criminal legislation, we may safely declare that this statute was not intended to apply to cases of self-defense.

When the rationale of the excuse of self-defense is thus explained, it becomes apparent that precisely the same reasoning is applicable to the case at bar. If in the future any group of men ever find themselves in the tragic predicament of these defendants, we may be sure that their decision whether to live or die will not be controlled by the contents of our criminal code. Accordingly, if we read this statute intelligently, it is apparent that it does not apply to this case. The withdrawal of this situation from the effect of the statute is justified by precisely the same considerations that were applied by our predecessors in office centuries ago to the case of self-defense.

There are those who raise the cry of judicial usurpation whenever a court, after analyzing the purpose of a statute, gives to its words a meaning that is not at once apparent to the casual reader who has not studied the statute closely or examined the objectives it seeks to attain. Let me say emphatically that I accept without reservation the proposition that this Court is bound by the statutes of our Commonwealth and that it exercises its powers in subservience to the duly expressed will of the Chamber of Representatives. The line of reasoning I have applied above raises no question of fidelity to enacted law, though it may possibly raise a question of the distinction between intelligent and unintelligent fidelity. No superior wants a servant who lacks the capacity to read between the lines. The stupidest housemaid knows that when she is told "to peel the soup and skim the potatoes" her mistress does not mean what she says. She also knows that when her master tells her to "drop everything and come running" he has overlooked the possibility that she is at the moment in the act of rescuing the baby from the rain barrel. Surely we have a right to expect the same modicum of intelligence from the judiciary. The correction of obvious legislative errors or oversights is not to supplant the legislative will, but to make that will effective.

I therefore conclude that on any aspect under which this case may be viewed these defendants are innocent of the crime of murdering Roger Whetmore, and that the conviction should be set aside.

OPINION OF JUSTICE TATTING

In the discharge of my duties as a justice of this Court, I am usually able to dissociate the emotional and intellectual sides of my reactions, and to decide the case before me entirely on the basis of the latter. In passing on this tragic case I find that my usual resources fail me. On the emotional side I find myself torn between sympathy for these men and a feeling of abhorrence and disgust at the monstrous act they committed. I had hoped that I would be able to put these contradictory emotions to one side as irrelevant, and to decide the case on the basis of a convincing and logical demonstration of the result demanded by our law. Unfortunately, this deliverance has not been vouchsafed me.

As I analyze the opinion just rendered by my brother Foster, I find that it is shot through with contradictions and fallacies. Let us begin with his first proposition: these men were not subject to our law because they were not in a "state of civil society" but in a "state of nature." I am not clear why this is so, whether it is because of the thickness of the rock that imprisoned them, or because they were hungry, or because they had set up a "new charter of government" by which the usual rules of law were to be supplanted by a throw of the dice. Other difficulties intrude themselves. If these men passed from the jurisdiction of our law to that of "the law of nature," at what moment did this occur? Was it when the entrance to the cave was blocked, or when the threat of starvation reached a certain undefined degree of intensity, or when the agreement for the throwing of the dice was made? These uncertainties in the doctrine proposed by my brother are capable of producing real difficulties. Suppose, for example, one of these men had had his twenty-first birthday while he was imprisoned within the mountain. On what date would we have to consider that he had attained his majority – when he reached the age of twenty-one, at which time he was, by hypothesis, removed from the effects of our law, or only when he was released from the cave and became again subject to what my brother calls our "positive law"? These difficulties may seem fanciful, yet they only serve to reveal the fanciful nature of the doctrine that is capable of giving rise to them.

But it is not necessary to explore these niceties further to demonstrate the absurdity of my brother's position. Mr Justice Foster and I are the appointed judges of a court of the Commonwealth of Newgarth, sworn and empowered to administer the laws of that Commonwealth. By what authority do we resolve ourselves into a Court of Nature? If these men were indeed under the law of nature, whence comes our authority to expound and apply that law? Certainly *we* are not in a state of nature.

Let us look at the contents of this code of nature that my brother proposes we adopt as our own and apply to this case. What a topsy-turvy and odious code it is! It is a code in which the law of contracts is more fundamental than the law of murder. It is a code under which a man may make a valid agreement empowering his fellows to eat his own body. Under the provisions of this code, furthermore, such an agreement once made is irrevocable, and if one of the parties attempts to withdraw, the others may take the law into their own hands and enforce the contract by violence – for though my brother passes over in convenient silence the effect of Whetmore's withdrawal, this is the necessary implication of his argument.

The principles my brother expounds contain other implications that cannot be tolerated. He argues that when the defendants set upon Whetmore and killed him (we know not how, perhaps by pounding him with stones) they were only exercising the rights conferred upon them by their bargain. Suppose, however, that Whetmore had had concealed upon his person a revolver, and that when he saw the defendants about to slaughter him he had shot them to death in order to save his own life. My brother's reasoning applied to these facts would make Whetmore out to be a murderer, since the excuse of self-defense would have to be denied to him. If his assailants were acting rightfully in seeking to bring about his death, then of course he could no more plead the excuse that he was defending his own life than could a condemned prisoner who struck down the executioner lawfully attempting to place the noose about his neck.

All of these considerations make it impossible for me to accept the first part of my brother's argument. I can neither accept his notion that these men were under a code of nature which this Court was bound to apply to them, nor can I accept the odious and perverted rules that he would read into that code. I come now to the second part of my brother's opinion, in which he seeks to show that the defendants did not violate the provisions of N.C.S.A. (N.S.) §12-A. Here the way, instead of being clear, becomes for me misty and ambiguous, though my brother seems unaware of the difficulties that inhere in his demonstrations.

The gist of my brother's argument may be stated in the following terms: No statute, whatever its language, should be applied in a way that contradicts its purpose. One of the purposes of any criminal statute is to deter. The application of the statute making it a crime to kill another to the peculiar facts of this case would contradict this purpose, for it is impossible to believe that the contents of the criminal code could operate in a deterrent manner on men faced with the alternative of life or death. The reasoning by which this exception is read into the statute is, my brother observes, the same as that which is applied in order to provide the excuse of self-defense.

On the face of things this demonstration seems very convincing indeed. My

16

brother's interpretation of the rationale of the excuse of self-defense is in fact supported by a decision of this court, *Commonwealth v. Parry*, a precedent I happened to encounter in my research on this case. Though *Commonwealth v. Parry* seems generally to have been overlooked in the texts and subsequent decisions, it supports unambiguously the interpretation my brother has put upon the excuse of self-defense.

Now let me outline briefly, however, the perplexities that assail me when I examine my brother's demonstration more closely. It is true that a statute should be applied in the light of its purpose, and that *one* of the purposes of criminal legislation is recognized to be deterrence. The difficulty is that other purposes are also ascribed to the law of crimes. It has been said that one of its objects is to provide an orderly outlet for the instinctive human demand for retribution: *Commonwealth v. Scape*. It has also been said that its object is the rehabilitation of the wrongdoer: *Commonwealth v. Makeover*. Other theories have been propounded. Assuming that we must interpret a statute in the light of its purpose, what are we to do when it has many purposes or when its purposes are disputed?

A similar difficulty is presented by the fact that, although there is authority for my brother's interpretation of the excuse of self-defense, there is other authority which assigns to that excuse a different rationale. Indeed, until I happened on *Commonwealth v. Parry* I had never heard of the explanation given by my brother. The taught doctrine of our law schools, memorized by generations of law students, runs in the following terms: The statute concerning murder requires a "willful" act. The man who acts to repel an aggressive threat to his own life does not act "willfully," but in response to an impulse deeply ingrained in human nature. I suspect that there is hardly a lawyer in this Commonwealth who is not familiar with this line of reasoning, especially since the point is a great favorite of the bar examiners.

Now the familiar explanation for the excuse of self-defense just expounded obviously cannot be applied by analogy to the facts of this case. These men acted not only "willfully" but with great deliberation and after hours of discussing what they should do. Again we encounter a forked path, with one line of reasoning leading us in one direction and another in a direction that is exactly the opposite. This perplexity is in this case compounded, as it were, for we have to set off one explanation, incorporated in a virtually unknown precedent of this Court, against another explanation, which forms a part of the taught legal tradition of our law schools, but which, so far as I know, has never been adopted in any judicial decision.

I recognize the relevance of the precedents cited by my brother concerning the displaced "not" and the defendant who parked over time. But what are we to do with one of the landmarks of our jurisprudence, which again my brother passes over in silence? This is *Commonwealth v. Valjean*. Though the case is somewhat obscurely reported, it appears that the defendant was indicted for the larceny of a loaf of bread, and offered as a defense that he was in a condition approaching starvation. The court refused to accept this defense. If hunger cannot justify the theft of wholesome and natural food, how can it justify the killing and eating of a man? Again, if we look at the thing in terms of deterrence, is it likely that a man will starve to death to avoid a jail sentence for the theft of a loaf of bread? My brother's demonstrations would compel us to overrule *Commonwealth v. Valjean*, and many other precedents that have been built on that case.

Again, I have difficulty in saying that no deterrent effect whatever could be attributed to a decision that these men were guilty of murder. The stigma of the word "murderer" is such that it is quite likely, I believe, that if these men had known that their act was deemed by the law to be murder they would have waited for a few days at least before carrying out their plan. During that time some unexpected relief might have come. I realize that this observation only reduces the distinction to a matter of degree, and does not destroy it altogether. It is certainly true that the element of deterrence would be less in this case than is normally involved in the application of the criminal law.

There is still a further difficulty in my brother Foster's proposal to read an exception into the statute to favor this case, though again a difficulty not even intimated in his opinion. What shall be the scope of this exception? Here the men cast lots and the victim was himself originally a party to the agreement. What would we have to decide if Whetmore had refused from the beginning to participate in the plan? Would a majority be permitted to overrule him? Or, suppose that no plan were adopted at all and the others simply conspired to bring about Whetmore's death, justifying their act by saying that he was in the weakest condition. Or again, that a plan of selection was followed but one based on a different justification than the one adopted here, as if the others were atheists and insisted that Whetmore should die because he was the only one who believed in an afterlife. These illustrations could be multiplied, but enough have been suggested to reveal what a quagmire of hidden difficulties my brother's reasoning contains.

Of course I realize on reflection that I may be concerning myself with a problem that will never arise, since it is unlikely that any group of men will ever again be brought to commit the dread act that was involved here. Yet, on still further reflection, even if we are certain that no similar case will arise again, do not the illustrations I have given show the lack of any coherent and rational principle in the rule my brother proposes? Should not the soundness of a principle be tested by the conclusions it entails, without reference to the accidents of later litigational history? Still, if this is so, why is it that we of this Court so often discuss the question whether we are likely to have later occasion to apply a principle urged for the solution of the case before us? Is this a situation where a line of reasoning not originally proper has become sanctioned by precedent, so that we are permitted to apply it and may even be under an obligation to do so?

The more I examine this case and think about it, the more deeply I become involved. My mind becomes entangled in the meshes of the very nets I throw out for my own rescue. I find that almost every consideration that bears on the decision of the case is counterbalanced by an opposing consideration leading in the opposite direction. My brother Foster has not furnished to me, nor can I discover for myself, any formula capable of resolving the equivocations that beset me on all sides.

I have given this case the best thought of which I am capable. I have scarcely slept since it was argued before us. When I feel myself inclined to accept the view of my brother Foster, I am repelled by a feeling that his arguments are intellectually unsound and approach mere rationalization. On the other hand, when I incline toward upholding the conviction, I am struck by the absurdity of directing that these men be put to death when their lives have been saved at the cost of the lives of ten heroic workmen. It is to me a matter of regret that the Prosecutor saw fit to ask for an indictment for murder. If we had a provision in our statutes making it a crime to eat human flesh, that would have been a more appropriate charge. If no other charge suited to the facts of this case could be brought against the defendants, it would have been wiser, I think, not to have indicted them at all. Unfortunately, however, the men have been indicted and tried, and we have therefore been drawn into this unfortunate affair.

Since I have been wholly unable to resolve the doubts that beset me about the law of this case, I am with regret announcing a step that is, I believe, unprecedented in the history of this tribunal. I declare my withdrawal from the decision of this case.

OPINION OF JUSTICE KEEN

I should like to begin by setting to one side two questions which are not before this Court.

The first of these is whether executive clemency should be extended to these defendants if the conviction is affirmed. Under our system of government, that is a question for the Chief Executive, not for us. I therefore disapprove of that passage in the opinion of the Chief Justice in which he in effect gives instructions to the Chief Executive as to what he should do in this case and suggests that some impropriety will attach if these instructions are not heeded. This is a confusion of governmental functions – a confusion of which the judiciary should be the last to be guilty. I wish to state that if I were the Chief Executive I would go farther in the direction of clemency than the pleas addressed to him propose. I would pardon these men altogether, since I believe that they have already suffered enough to pay for any offense they may have committed. I want it to be understood that this remark is made in my capacity as a private citizen who by the accident of his office happens to have acquired an intimate acquaintance with the facts of this case. In the discharge of my duties as judge, it is neither my function to address directions to the Chief Executive, nor to take into account what he may or may not do, in reaching my own decision, which must be controlled entirely by the law of this Commonwealth.

The second question that I wish to put to one side is that of deciding whether what these men did was "right" or "wrong," "wicked" or "good." That is also a question that is irrelevant to the discharge of my office as a judge sworn to apply, not my conceptions of morality, but the law of the land. In putting this question to one side I think I can also safely dismiss without comment the first and more poetic portion of my brother Foster's opinion. The element of fantasy contained in the arguments developed there has been sufficiently revealed in my brother Tatting's somewhat solemn attempt to take those arguments seriously.

The sole question before us for decision is whether these defendants did, within the meaning of N.C.S.A. (N.S.) §12-A, willfully take the life of Roger Whetmore. The exact language of the statute is as follows: "Whoever shall willfully take the life of another shall be punished by death." Now I should suppose that any candid observer, content to extract from these words their natural meaning, would concede at once that these defendants did "willfully take the life" of Roger Whetmore.

Whence arise all the difficulties of the case, then, and the necessity for so many pages of discussion about what ought to be so obvious? The difficulties, in whatever tortured form they may present themselves, all trace back to a single source, and that is a failure to distinguish the legal from the moral aspects of this case. To put it bluntly, my brothers do not like the fact that the written law requires the conviction of these defendants. Neither do I, but unlike my brothers I respect the obligations of an office that requires me to put my personal predilections out of my mind when I come to interpret and apply the law of this Commonwealth.

Now, of course, my brother Foster does not admit that he is actuated by a personal dislike of the written law. Instead he develops a familiar line of argument according to which the court may disregard the express language of a statute when something not contained in the statute itself, called its "purpose," can be employed to justify the result the court considers proper. Because this is an old issue between myself and my colleague, I should like, before discussing his particular application of the argument to the facts of this case, to say something about the historical background of this issue and its implications for law and government generally.

There was a time in this Commonwealth when judges did in fact legislate very freely, and all of us know that during that period some of our statutes were rather thoroughly made over by the judiciary. That was a time when the accepted principles of political science did not designate with any certainty the rank and function of the various arms of the state. We all know the tragic issue of that uncertainty in the brief civil war that arose out of the conflicts between the judiciary, on the one hand, and the executive and the legislature, on the other. There is no need to recount here the factors that contributed to that unseemly struggle for power, though they included the unrepresentative character of the Chamber, resulting from a division of the country into election districts that no longer accorded with the actual distribution of the population, and the forceful personality and wide popular following of the then Chief Justice. It is enough to observe that those days are behind us, and that in place of the uncertainty that then reigned we now have a clear-cut principle, which is the supremacy of the legislative branch of our government. From that principle flows the obligation of the judiciary to enforce faithfully the written law, and to interpret that law in accordance with its plain meaning without reference to our personal desires or our individual conceptions of justice. I am not concerned with the question whether the principle that forbids the judicial revision of statutes is right or wrong, desirable or undesirable; I observe merely that this principle has become a tacit premise underlying the whole of the legal and governmental order I am sworn to administer.

Yet though the principle of the supremacy of the legislature has been accepted in theory for centuries, such is the tenacity of professional tradition and the force of fixed habits of thought that many of the judiciary have still not accommodated themselves to the restricted role which the new order imposes on them. My brother Foster is one of that group; his way of dealing with statutes is exactly that of a judge living in the 3900s.

We are all familiar with the process by which the judicial reform of disfavored legislative enactments is accomplished. Anyone who has followed the written opinions of Mr Justice Foster will have had an opportunity to see it at work in every branch of the law. I am personally so familiar with the process that in the event of my brother's incapacity I am sure I could write a satisfactory opinion for him without any prompting whatever, beyond being informed whether he liked the effect of the terms of the statute as applied to the case before him.

The process of judicial reform requires three steps. The first of these is to divine some single "purpose" which the statute serves. This is done although not one statute in a hundred has any such single purpose, and although the objectives of nearly every statute are differently interpreted by the different classes of its sponsors. The second step is to discover that a mythical being called "the legislator," in the pursuit of this imagined "purpose," overlooked something or left some gap or imperfection in his work. Then comes the final and most refreshing part of the task, which is, of course, to fill in the blank thus created. *Quod erat faciendum* [which was to be done].

My brother Foster's penchant for finding holes in statutes reminds one of the story told by an ancient author about the man who ate a pair of shoes. Asked how he liked them, he replied that the part he liked best was the holes. That is the way my brother feels about statutes; the more holes they have in them the better he likes them. In short, he doesn't like statutes.

One could not wish for a better case to illustrate the specious nature of this gap-filling process than the one before us. My brother thinks he knows exactly what was sought when men made murder a crime, and that was something he calls "deterrence." My brother Tatting has already shown how much is passed over in that interpretation. But I think the trouble goes deeper. I doubt very much whether our statute making murder a crime really has a "purpose" in any ordinary sense of the term. Primarily, such a statute reflects a deeply-felt human conviction that murder is wrong and that something should be done to the man who commits it. If we were forced to be more articulate about the matter, we would probably take refuge in the more sophisticated theories of the criminologists, which, of course, were certainly not in the minds of those who drafted our statute. We might also observe that men will do their own work more effectively and live happier lives if they are protected against the threat of violent assault. Bearing in mind that the victims of murders are often unpleasant people, we might add some suggestion that the matter of disposing of undesirables is not a function suited to private enterprise, but should be a state monopoly. All of which reminds me of the attorney who once argued before us that a statute licensing physicians was a good thing because it would lead to lower life insur-

ance rates by lifting the level of general health. There is such a thing as over-explaining the obvious.

If we do not know the purpose of §12-A, how can we possibly say there is a "gap" in it? How can we know what its draftsmen thought about the question of killing men in order to eat them? My brother Tatting has revealed an understandable, though perhaps slightly exaggerated, revulsion to cannibalism. How do we know that his remote ancestors did not feel the same revulsion to an even higher degree? Anthropologists say that the dread felt for a forbidden act may be increased by the fact that the conditions of a tribe's life create special temptations toward it, as incest is most severely condemned among those whose village relations make it most likely to occur. Certainly the period following the Great Spiral was one that had implicit in it temptations to anthropophagy. Perhaps it was for that very reason that our ancestors expressed their prohibition in so broad and unqualified a form. All of this is conjecture, of course, but it remains abundantly clear that neither I nor my brother Foster knows what the "purpose" of §12-A is.

Considerations similar to those I have just outlined are also applicable to the exception in favor of self-defense, which plays so large a role in the reasoning of my brothers Foster and Tatting. It is of course true that in *Commonwealth v. Parry* an *obiter dictum* justified this exception on the assumption that the purpose of criminal legislation is to deter. It may well also be true that generations of law students have been taught that the true explanation of the exception lies in the fact that a man who acts in self-defense does not act "willfully," and that the same students have passed their bar examinations by repeating what their professors told them. These last observations I could dismiss, of course, as irrelevant for the simple reason that professors and bar examiners have not as yet any commission to make our laws for us. But again the real trouble lies deeper. As in dealing with the statute, so in dealing with the exception, the question is not the conjectural *purpose* of the rule, but its *scope*. Now the scope of the exception in favor of self-defense as it has been applied by this Court is plain: it applies to cases of resisting an aggressive threat to the party's own life. It is therefore too clear for argument that this case does not fall within the scope of the exception, since it is plain that Whetmore made no threat against the lives of these defendants.

The essential shabbiness of my brother Foster's attempt to cloak his remaking of the written law with an air of legitimacy comes tragically to the surface in my brother Tatting's opinion. In that opinion Justice Tatting struggles manfully to combine his colleague's loose moralisms with his own sense of fidelity to the written law. The issue of this struggle could only be that which occurred, a complete default in the discharge of the judicial function. You simply cannot apply a statute as it is written and remake it to meet your own wishes at the same time.

Now I know that the line of reasoning I have developed in this opinion will not be acceptable to those who look only to the immediate effects of a decision

and ignore the long-run implications of an assumption by the judiciary of a power of dispensation. A hard decision is never a popular decision. Judges have been celebrated in literature for their sly prowess in devising some quibble by which a litigant could be deprived of his rights where the public thought it was wrong for him to assert those rights. But I believe that judicial dispensation does more harm in the long run than hard decisions. Hard cases may even have a certain moral value by bringing home to the people their own responsibilities toward the law that is ultimately their creation, and by reminding them that there is no principle of personal grace that can relieve the mistakes of their representatives.

Indeed, I will go farther and say that not only are the principles I have been expounding those which are soundest for our present conditions, but that we would have inherited a better legal system from our forefathers if those principles had been observed from the beginning. For example, with respect to the excuse of self-defense, if our courts had stood steadfast on the language of the statute the result would undoubtedly have been a legislative revision of it. Such a revision would have drawn on the assistance of natural philosophers and psychologists, and the resulting regulation of the matter would have had an understandable and rational basis, instead of the hodgepodge of verbalisms and metaphysical distinctions that have emerged from the judicial and professorial treatment.

These concluding remarks are, of course, beyond any duties that I have to discharge with relation to this case, but I include them here because I feel deeply that my colleagues are insufficiently aware of the dangers implicit in the conceptions of the judicial office advocated by my brother Foster.

I conclude that the conviction should be affirmed.

OPINION OF JUSTICE HANDY

I have listened with amazement to the tortured ratiocinations to which this simple case has given rise. I never cease to wonder at my colleagues' ability to throw an obscuring curtain of legalisms about every issue presented to them for decision. We have heard this afternoon learned disquisitions on the distinction between positive law and the law of nature, the language of the statute and the purpose of the statute, judicial functions and executive functions, judicial legislation and legislative legislation. My only disappointment was that someone did not raise the question of the legal nature of the bargain struck in the cave – whether it was unilateral or bilateral, and whether Whetmore could not be considered as having revoked an offer prior to action taken thereunder.

What have all these things to do with the case? The problem before us is what we, as officers of the government, ought to do with these defendants. That is a question of practical wisdom, to be exercised in a context, not of abstract theory, but of human realities. When the case is approached in this light, it becomes, I think, one of the easiest to decide that has ever been argued before this Court.

Before stating my own conclusions about the merits of the case, I should like to discuss briefly some of the more fundamental issues involved – issues on which my colleagues and I have been divided ever since I have been on the bench.

I have never been able to make my brothers see that government is a human affair, and that men are ruled, not by words on paper or by abstract theories, but by other men. They are ruled well when their rulers understand the feelings and conceptions of the masses. They are ruled badly when that understanding is lacking.

Of all branches of the government, the judiciary is the most likely to lose its contact with the common man. The reasons for this are, of course, fairly obvious. Where the masses react to a situation in terms of a few salient features, we pick into little pieces every situation presented to us. Lawyers are hired by both sides to analyze and dissect. Judges and attorneys vie with one another to see who can discover the greatest number of difficulties and distinctions in a single set of facts. Each side tries to find cases, real or imagined, that will embarrass the demonstrations of the other side. To escape this embarrassment, still further distinctions are invented and imported into the situation. When a set of facts has been subjected to this kind of treatment for a sufficient time, all the life and juice have gone out of it and we have left a handful of dust.

Now I realize that wherever you have rules and abstract principles lawyers are going to be able to make distinctions. To some extent the sort of thing I have been describing is a necessary evil attaching to any formal regulation of human affairs. But I think that the area which really stands in need of such regulation is greatly overestimated. There are, of course, a few fundamental rules of the game that must be accepted if the game is to go on at all. I would include among these the rules relating to the conduct of elections, the appointment of public officials, and the term during which an office is held. Here some restraint on discretion and dispensation, some adherence to form, some scruple for what does and what does not fall within the rule, is, I concede, essential. Perhaps the area of basic principle should be expanded to include certain other rules, such as those designed to preserve the free civilmoign system.

But outside of these fields I believe that all government officials, including judges, will do their jobs best if they treat forms and abstract concepts as instruments. We should take as our model, I think, the good administrator, who accommodates procedures and principles to the case at hand, selecting from among the available forms those most suited to reach the proper result.

The most obvious advantage of this method of government is that it permits us to go about our daily tasks with efficiency and common sense. My adherence to this philosophy has, however, deeper roots. I believe that it is only with the insight this philosophy gives that we can preserve the flexibility essential if we are to keep our actions in reasonable accord with the sentiments of those subject to our rule. More governments have been wrecked, and more human misery caused, by the lack of this accord between ruler and ruled than by any other factor that can be discerned in history. Once drive a sufficient wedge between the mass of people and those who direct their legal, political, and economic life, and our society is ruined. Then neither Foster's law of nature nor Keen's fidelity to written law will avail us anything.

Now when these conceptions are applied to the case before us, its decision becomes, as I have said, perfectly easy. In order to demonstrate this I shall have to introduce certain realities that my brothers in their coy decorum have seen fit to pass over in silence, although they are just as acutely aware of them as I am.

The first of these is that this case has aroused an enormous public interest, both here and abroad. Almost every newspaper and magazine has carried articles about it; columnists have shared with their readers confidential information as to the next governmental move; hundreds of letters-to-the-editor have been printed. One of the great newspaper chains made a poll of public opinion on the question, "What do you think the Supreme Court should do with the Speluncean explorers?" About ninety per cent expressed a belief that the defendants should be pardoned or let off with a kind of token punishment. It is perfectly clear, then, how the public feels about the case. We could have known this without the poll, of course, on the basis of common sense, or even by observing that on this Court there are apparently four-and-a-half men, or ninety per cent, who share the common opinion.

This makes it obvious, not only what we should do, but what we must do if we are to preserve between ourselves and public opinion a reasonable and decent accord. Declaring these men innocent need not involve us in any undignified quibble or trick. No principle of statutory construction is required that is not consistent with the past practices of this Court. Certainly no layman would think that in letting these men off we had stretched the statute any more than our ancestors did when they created the excuse of self-defense. If a more detailed demonstration of the method of reconciling our decision with the statute is required, I should be content to rest on the arguments developed in the second and less visionary part of my brother Foster's opinion.

Now I know that my brothers will be horrified by my suggestion that this Court should take account of public opinion. They will tell you that public opinion is emotional and capricious, that it is based on half-truths and listens to witnesses who are not subject to cross-examination. They will tell you that the law surrounds the trial of a case like this with elaborate safeguards, designed to insure that the truth will be known and that every rational consideration bearing on the issues of the case has been taken into account. They will warn you that all of these safeguards go for naught if a mass opinion formed outside this framework is allowed to have any influence on our decision.

But let us look candidly at some of the realities of the administration of our criminal law. When a man is accused of crime, there are, speaking generally, four ways in which he may escape punishment. One of these is a determination by a judge that under the applicable law he has committed no crime. This is, of course, a determination that takes place in a rather formal and abstract atmosphere. But look at the other three ways in which he may escape punishment. These are: (1) a decision by the Prosecutor not to ask for an indictment; (2) an acquittal by the jury; (3) a pardon or commutation of sentence by the executive. Can anyone pretend that these decisions are held within a rigid and formal framework of rules that prevents factual error, excludes emotional and personal factors, and guarantees that all the forms of the law will be observed?

In the case of the jury we do, to be sure, attempt to cabin their deliberations within the area of the legally relevant, but there is no need to deceive ourselves into believing that this attempt is really successful. In the normal course of events the case now before us would have gone on all of its issues directly to the jury. Had this occurred we can be confident that there would have been an acquittal or at least a division that would have prevented a conviction. If the jury had been instructed that the men's hunger and their agreement were no defense to the charge of murder, their verdict would in all likelihood have ignored this instruction and would have involved a good deal more twisting of the letter of the law than any that is likely to tempt us. Of course the only reason that didn't occur in this case was the fortuitous circumstance that the foreman of the jury happened to be a lawyer. His learning enabled him to devise a form of words that would allow the jury to dodge its usual responsibilities.

My brother Tatting expresses annoyance that the Prosecutor did not, in effect, decide the case for him by not asking for an indictment. Strict as he is himself in complying with the demands of legal theory, he is quite content to have the fate of these men decided out of court by the Prosecutor on the basis of common sense. The Chief Justice, on the other hand, wants the application of common sense postponed to the very end, though, like Tatting, he wants no personal part in it.

This brings me to the concluding portion of my remarks, which has to do with executive clemency. Before discussing that topic directly, I want to make a related observation about the poll of public opinion. As I have said, ninety per cent of the people wanted the Supreme Court to let the men off entirely or with a more or less nominal punishment. The ten per cent constituted a very oddly assorted group, with the most curious and divergent opinions. One of our university experts has made a study of this group and has found that its members fall into certain patterns. A substantial portion of them are subscribers to "crank" newspapers of limited circulation that gave their readers a distorted version of the facts of the case. Some thought that "Speluncean" means "cannibal" and that anthropophagy is a tenet of the Society. But the point I want to make, however, is this: although almost every conceivable variety and shade of opinion was represented in this group, there was, so far as I know, not one of them, nor a single member of the majority of ninety per cent, who said, "I think it would be a fine thing to have the courts sentence these men to be hanged, and then to have another branch of the government come along and pardon them." Yet this is a solution that has more or less dominated our discussions and which our Chief Justice proposes as a way by which we can avoid doing an injustice and at the same time preserve respect for law. He can be assured that if he is preserving anybody's morale, it is his own, and not the public's, which knows nothing of his distinctions. I mention this matter because I wish to emphasize once more the danger that we may get lost in the patterns of our own thought and forget that these patterns often cast not the slightest shadow on the outside world.

I come now to the most crucial fact in this case, a fact known to all of us on this Court, though one that my brothers have seen fit to keep under the cover of their judicial robes. This is the frightening likelihood that if the issue is left to him, the Chief Executive will refuse to pardon these men or commute their sentence. As we all know, our Chief Executive is a man now well advanced in years, of very stiff notions. Public clamor usually operates on him with the reverse of the effect intended. As I have told my brothers, it happens that my wife's niece is an intimate friend of his secretary. I have learned in this indirect, but, I think, wholly reliable way, that he is firmly determined not to commute the sentence if these men are found to have violated the law.

No one regrets more than I the necessity for relying in so important a matter on information that could be characterized as gossip. If I had my way this would not happen, for I would adopt the sensible course of sitting down with the Executive, going over the case with him, finding out what his views are, and perhaps working out with him a common program for handling the situation. But of course my brothers would never hear of such a thing.

Their scruple about acquiring accurate information directly does not prevent them from being very perturbed about what they have learned indirectly. Their acquaintance with the facts I have just related explains why the Chief Justice, ordinarily a model of decorum, saw fit in his opinion to flap his judicial robes in the face of the Executive and threaten him with excommunication if he failed to commute the sentence. It explains, I suspect, my brother Foster's feat of levitation by which a whole library of law books was lifted from the shoulders of these defendants. It explains also why even my legalistic brother Keen emulated Pooh-Bah in the ancient comedy by stepping to the other side of the stage to address a few remarks to the Executive "in my capacity as a private citizen." (I may remark, incidentally, that the advice of Private Citizen Keen will appear in the reports of this Court printed at taxpayers' expense.)

I must confess that as I grow older I become more and more perplexed at men's refusal to apply their common sense to problems of law and government, and this truly tragic case has deepened my sense of discouragement and dismay. I only wish that I could convince my brothers of the wisdom of the principles I have applied to the judicial office since I first assumed it. As a matter of fact, by a kind of sad rounding of the circle, I encountered issues like those involved here in the very first case I tried as Judge of the Court of General Instances in Fanleigh County.

A religious sect had unfrocked a minister who, they said, had gone over to the views and practices of a rival sect. The minister circulated a handbill making charges against the authorities who had expelled him. Certain lay members of the church announced a public meeting at which they proposed to explain the position of the church. The minister attended this meeting. Some said he slipped in unobserved in a disguise; his own testimony was that he had walked in openly as a member of the public. At any rate, when the speeches began he interrupted with certain questions about the affairs of the church and made some statements in defense of his own views. He was set upon by members of the audience and given a pretty thorough pommeling, receiving among other injuries a broken jaw. He brought a suit for damages against the association that sponsored the meeting and against ten named individuals who he alleged were his assailants.

When we came to the trial, the case at first seemed very complicated to me. The attorneys raised a host of legal issues. There were nice questions on the admissibility of evidence, and, in connection with the suit against the association, some difficult problems turning on the question whether the minister was a trespasser or a licensee. As a novice on the bench I was eager to apply my law school learning and I began studying these questions closely, reading all the authorities and preparing well-documented rulings. As I studied the case I became more and more involved in its legal intricacies and I began to get into a state approaching that of my brother Tatting in this case. Suddenly, however, it dawned on me that all these perplexing issues really had nothing to do with the case, and I began examining it in the light of common sense. The case at once gained a new perspective, and I saw that the only thing for me to do was to direct a verdict for the defendants for lack of evidence.

I was led to this conclusion by the following considerations. The mêlée in which the plaintiff was injured had been a very confused affair, with some people trying to get to the center of the disturbance, while others were trying to get away from it; some striking at the plaintiff, while others were apparently trying to protect him. It would have taken weeks to find out the truth of the matter. I decided that nobody's broken jaw was worth that much to the Commonwealth. (The minister's injuries, incidentally, had meanwhile healed without disfigurement and without any impairment of normal faculties.) Furthermore, I felt very strongly that the plaintiff had to a large extent brought the thing on himself. He knew how inflamed passions were about the affair, and could easily have found another forum for the expression of his views. My decision was widely approved by the press and public opinion, neither of which could tolerate the views and practices that the expelled minister was attempting to defend.

Now, thirty years later, thanks to an ambitious Prosecutor and a legalistic jury foreman, I am faced with a case that raises issues which are at bottom much like those involved in that case. The world does not seem to change much, except that this time it is not a question of a judgment for five or six hundred frelars, but of the life or death of four men who have already suffered more torment and humiliation than most of us would endure in a thousand years. I conclude that the defendants are innocent of the crime charged, and that the conviction and sentence should be set aside.

OPINION OF JUSTICE TATTING

I have been asked by the Chief Justice whether, after listening to the two opinions just rendered, I desire to re-examine the position previously taken by me. I wish to state that after hearing these opinions I am greatly strengthened in my conviction that I ought not to participate in the decision of this case.

The Supreme Court being evenly divided, the conviction and sentence of the Court of General Instances is *affirmed*. It is ordered that the execution of the sentence shall occur at 6 a.m., Friday, April 2, 4300, at which time the Public Executioner is directed to proceed with all convenient dispatch to hang each of the defendants by the neck until he is dead.

POSTSCRIPT

Now that the court has spoken its judgment, the reader puzzled by the choice of date may wish to be reminded that the centuries which separate us from the year 4300 are roughly equal to those that have passed since the Age of Pericles. There is probably no need to observe that the *Speluncean Case* itself is intended neither as a work of satire nor as a prediction in any ordinary sense of the term. As for the judges who make up Chief Justice Truepenny's court, they are, of course, as mythical as the facts and precedents with which they deal. The reader who refuses to accept this view, and who seeks to trace out contemporary resemblances where none is intended or contemplated, should be warned that he is engaged in a frolic of his own, which may possibly lead him to miss whatever modest truths are contained in the opinions delivered by the Supreme Court of Newgarth. The case was constructed for the sole purpose of bringing into a common focus certain divergent philosophies of law and government. These philosophies presented men with live questions of choice in the days of Plato and Aristotle. Perhaps they will continue to do so when our era has had its say about them. If there is any element of prediction in the case, it does not go beyond a suggestion that the questions involved are among the permanent problems of the human race.

Lon L. Fuller

Part II

NINE NEW OPINIONS
In the Supreme Court of Newgarth, 4350

OPINION OF CHIEF JUSTICE
BURNHAM

I

The world was taken by surprise late last year when an elderly man living alone in our western wilderness was arrested by provincial police and charged with a fifty-year-old murder. He did not deny that he and four friends had once killed a man, but he did deny that their action amounted to murder. He confessed to being the sixth member of the party of speluncean explorers trapped in a land-slide fifty years earlier and forced by starvation, as it seemed to them, to kill and eat one of their companions. Of the five survivors of that tragic adventure, four were captured, tried, and convicted of murder. They gave no hint at trial that a living, fifth survivor was then at large or had ever been in the cave with them. This Court reviewed their conviction, *Commonwealth v. Spelunkers* (hereafter, *Spelunkers I*). An evenly divided Court let the jury conviction stand. The four defendants were duly executed.

The present defendant has admitted to all the facts established in the trial of his four comrades. These are ably summarized by Chief Justice Truepenny in *Spelunkers I* (at pp. 7f, above). The defendant has refused to elaborate where that factual record is silent, for example on the mathematical details discussed when planning the lottery, or the exact method of killing. The only new facts he has provided pertain to his escape. Interesting as these are, they do not bear on the question whether he is guilty of murder. Because he absconded from the rescue camp before he was arrested, he was not charged with escaping custody.

The western provincial prosecutor charged him only with murder and a jury convicted him.

The murder statute in Newgarth today is identical to the murder statute fifty years ago: "Whoever shall willfully take the life of another shall be punished by death," N.C.S.A. (N.S.) §12-A. Indeed, *Spelunkers I* inspired at least two proposals to amend this statute, the first to elaborate on what shall count as willfulness and the second to give judges some discretion to select a fitting punishment. But both proposals were defeated. Legislators defended the current, and venerable, murder statute for its stark simplicity. This simplicity, they argued, gives little support to hair-splitting, and makes it easy for citizens to understand the law and to apply it to their own conduct. For all these reasons, the statute remains unmodified. Hence the present defendant was convicted under the same standard as his comrades, for the same act as his comrades.

He appealed his conviction to the Western Circuit Court of Appeals, which decided against him, citing *Spelunkers I* as precedent. He now appeals to us. We find ourselves, therefore, in the unusual position of ruling on a case factually and legally identical to one long since closed. The prior case was fully litigated on the merits, and all appeals were exhausted. These would be good reasons to deny review in the present case and let the appellate decision stand. But the Court of Appeals misunderstood the nature and force of the precedent. *Spelunkers I* is not a decision upholding the jury conviction; it is a non-decision with no majority and no two judges in agreement. It did not affirm the guilt of the four defendants; it failed to find a majority willing to affirm or deny that guilt, with the procedural effect of leaving the jury verdict undisturbed. The Court of Appeals was tempted, as we were, to avoid rehearing a case whose disposition has both legal and historical finality. But by taking *Spelunkers I* for a decision on the merits with the force of precedent, the Court of Appeals erred. We took the present case in part to rectify that error. We also felt that these important facts deserve a more authoritative resolution than they received half a century ago. With hope that contemporary legal theory equips us for such a resolution, better than the schools of thought responsible for the judicial impasse fifty years ago, we accepted review. With that hope dashed, we issue our opinions today.

II

Justice Handy concluded *Spelunkers I* by appeal to public opinion and newspaper editorials. At that time, ninety per cent of the public wanted the four defendants acquitted (see p. 26, above). This figure is uncannily like the support enjoyed by the present defendant today. The public seems to believe that, morally, this is a simple case; I agree. The five surviving spelunkers did nothing that most good people would not have done in the same circumstances, but for the fact that most good people lack the courage and resolution of these five men. Even if the men did act immorally, it is hard to find a moral justification for executing them. If we condemn them for killing one man to save five, how can we justify killing ten workmen to bring them to trial in order only to kill them as well? The life of the fifth, before us today, is no easier to take than those of his companions.

But the public can be forgiven for thinking only of the morality of the case; we cannot. We must discover what the law requires.

Writing in *Spelunkers I*, Justices Truepenny and Keen argued that, legally, this is a simple case; I agree with this position as well. The spelunkers killed Whetmore willfully. There is no way to read the facts of this case and come to any other conclusion. The killing was premeditated. The method of selecting the victim was the object of a lengthy discussion. Every step was intentional. If at the last moment before his killers-to-be could crush his skull, Whetmore had stumbled, pitching head-first into a rock, and so had died, then surely the surviving spelunkers would have said so at trial. They could have said so anyway. The claim would have been suspicious but irrefutable. But, on the contrary, they introduced no evidence whatsoever to negate the conclusion that they voluntarily and intentionally killed Roger Whetmore.

So the case is an easy one morally and legally. Unfortunately, the morally easy verdict is acquittal and the legally easy verdict is conviction. This contradiction explains all the agony my colleagues display in their lengthy opinions.

But there is no need for agony or even length. We are justices of the Supreme Court who have taken oaths to interpret, apply, and uphold the laws of the Commonwealth of Newgarth. While the law is often unclear, the meaning of our oath is clear. When law and morality conflict, judges in their role as judges must follow the law. Judges in their role as citizens are free to do many other things, such as petition the executive for clemency, lobby the legislature for reform, criticize the prosecutor, second-guess the jury, write angry letters to the editor, kick the cat. As judges, we must follow the law. Since legally this is an easy case, deciding where our duty lies is equally easy. The previous defendants were guilty of murder; the present defendant is guilty of murder.

III

In short, I agree entirely with Justice Keen. However, Keen did not answer every objection raised by the defense at trial. The prosecutor tried, but the job can be done more systematically.

The defendant offers many objections to the holding of willful murder. While these objections have a legal color, they do not in my view have a legal origin. I believe they originate in legally irrelevant feelings of sympathy and personal views of morality.

I have above summarized the case for holding the killing of Whetmore to be willful. This seems to me overwhelming. Indeed, I am convinced that if an equally strong argument for willfulness appeared in another murder case where it was unopposed by legally irrelevant feelings of sympathy or personal views of morality, then every judge and every citizen in the land would find the defendant guilty in an instant.

For example, imagine a killer who undoubtedly lacks evil will, but who undoubtedly possesses intention, voluntariness, and premeditation, like these spelunkers. Imagine such a killer for whom we have no irrelevant feelings of personal sympathy. Imagine a rich man who learns by his car telephone about an exciting party one mile away. He is not dressed properly and has no time to go home or to purchase proper attire. So he cruises the street on which he finds himself until he sees a man his own size wearing a swank blazer and really elegant tie. He asks his chauffeur to pull over, and together they haul the man into the car, remove his coat and tie, and slice his throat with the sharp edge of an empty caviar can from the litter basket. Would any one doubt that this killing is *willful?* No. But if this killer possesses intention without ill-will, like the spelunkers, then the only reason we would convict him and acquit the spelunkers is a feeling of sympathy for the poor spelunkers, a feeling that may be common, natural, and admirable, but that has no authority whatsoever under our law.

However irrelevant these feelings may be, they have motivated many good lawyers to seek relevant legal objections to the otherwise conclusive case for willfulness. So while they are frivolous and tortured, these objections should be answered briefly for the record.

The present defendant, like his comrades before him, appeals primarily to what has been called the defense of necessity. He claims that necessity forced his hand. He claims further, that if so, then his act was not *willful* in the legal sense of that term. The statute tells us, of course, that if his act was not willful, then it was not murder. Let us examine these claims more closely.

1. If I can violate the law with impunity provided I claim that necessity forced my hand, then I can do whatever I wish. So can everyone else. The result is the direct and total subversion of the rule of law. If the necessity defense is to have legal force, then it must be severely restricted. At least the defendants who employ it must do more than claim necessity. They must do more, even, than show their belief in necessity to have been genuine or sincere. They must show that their belief in necessity was reasonable in the circumstances. They must show that there was an objective basis to believe that no other options were open to them.

I will grant that these spelunkers did believe that killing one of their friends was necessary. It is hard to imagine why they would kill a friend in the absence of such a belief. However, this was not a reasonable belief in the circumstances. Whetmore wanted to wait another week before killing anyone. If he thought they could last another week, even if he was mistaken, then the men could not have been pinched by true necessity on the day of the killing. Just as a single hold-out on a jury saves the defendant and triggers a mistrial, perhaps showing the existence of reasonable doubt, one starving spelunker willing to wait another week condemns the defendant and clinches the prosecution, showing that it is not reasonable to believe that immediate homicide is necessary for survival.

2. Even if the spelunkers did have a reasonable belief that killing one of their party was necessary, our decision in *Commonwealth v. Valjean* overturns their argument. We have long settled the question whether starvation counts as necessity; it does not. If a man cannot commit the relatively harmless act of stealing bread to avert starvation, then surely we cannot tolerate intentional homicide and cannibalism to avert starvation.

3. Even if starvation were the sort of necessity our law could recognize, and even if the spelunkers had a reasonable belief that it was imminent, they had a duty to mitigate. That is, they had a duty to try any expedient less grave than killing before actually killing. They could, for example, have waited for the first

of them to die of starvation and eaten that one. That would have made killing entirely unnecessary. They could even have eaten their fingers, toes, and ear lobes, or drunk their blood. If they began by eating their smallest toes, for example, they could easily staunch the flow of blood with a tourniquet. The usual objection to a tourniquet – that it entails the loss of the extremity – is irrelevant if they would eat the extremity in any case, or if they would die without such a recourse. Such snacks would have given the spelunkers sustenance for several days, perhaps even to the tenth day after radio contact when the rescuers predicted success. At least the men could have asked the medical experts by radio whether such snacks could have helped them to live long enough to be rescued. At least they could have lasted a few days longer, perhaps to the point of genuine necessity.

Note that there are at least four alternatives to killing: (1) waiting for the weakest to die of natural causes, (2) eating inessential extremities, (3) trying the radio again, and (4) waiting a few more days. Of these, the suggestion that they eat parts of themselves is admittedly grotesque and ghastly; but when the alternative is killing a man, it becomes not only sensible, but obligatory. If the necessity defense means anything, it means that circumstances gave them no option less evil than the one they chose. These men were in no such situation on the day they killed Roger Whetmore.

4. Even if they had no duty to try less horrifying expedients before more horrifying ones, the necessity defense cannot be used by those for whom the danger or necessity arises from their own choice. These men assumed the risk of a landslide. Why else leave instructions with their club to come looking for them if they did not return by a certain date? Why else take a radio? They knew that the sport of cave exploration was dangerous and they made a free choice to expose themselves to its risks. They are to be pitied when the risks overtake them, but they have no legal complaint. They cannot take advantage of the danger they voluntarily faced in order to kill a man.

5. Even if they did not assume the risk of a landslide, they negligently brought too few provisions to meet the risk of a landslide. This is proved by the outcome. They knew the cave contained no animal or vegetable matter, yet they carried "only scant provisions" (see p. 7, above). We cannot blame them for the act of God that imprisoned them. But we can blame them for failing to equip themselves sufficiently to meet the risks they knew or should have known were inherent in their perilous sport.

6. Even if they are entitled to a full necessity defense, the victim must be chosen fairly. In this case the method of selection was the lottery to which they all at first consented. We do not know the mathematical details of the lottery on which they spent so much time. But clearly the time was well spent in the sense that they devised a method that won the consent of every member to a horrifying prospect. However, before the dice were thrown, Whetmore revoked his consent. His reason (as we noted above) was that he thought the lottery was not yet strictly necessary. While Whetmore's reason for revoking his consent cuts

against the necessity defense, his revocation itself, even if groundless or irrational, undermines the fairness of the selection process. When the selection method is unfair, then the overall defense collapses, even if the necessity component stands. Imagine a case with the same necessity as the present case; would we acquit the defendants if they had abandoned any attempt to pick a victim fairly, fell back instead on their racial animosities, and killed the one Euro-Newgarthian or Jew among them? Clearly not.

That is the end of the necessity defense in this case. It has not a leg to stand on.

IV

More than one of my colleagues has tried to replace the letter of the murder statute with its spirit, or to put the statute aside in order to fulfill its purpose. While our duty as judges requires us to interpret law, it does not permit us to remake clear law that we don't like and to call that act of usurpation "interpretation."

Under *Fehler*, we may remake a statute to correct an obvious typographical error. But that sound precedent cannot be stretched to acquit these spelunkers. In *Fehler*, the purpose of the statute was very clear; hence it served as a good guide to the proper reading of its corrupted language. In this case, as the disagreement of my colleagues proves, the purpose of our murder statute is not at all clear. It is either deterrence (*Parry*) or retribution (*Scape*) or rehabilitation (*Makeover*). We cannot build the edifice of law on such quicksand. Hence, we must live with the plain meaning of the statute and not refashion it to suit our tastes by appeal to controversial theories about its purpose.

Justice Tatting has argued that those who act to repel an aggressor do not act "willfully" because their response is rooted in a natural instinct (at p. 17, above). He does not apply this analysis to the spelunkers, because they obviously acted willfully, but he has nevertheless divined that the purpose of our murder statute is consonant with with human instinct. Similarly, Justice Foster admits that "self-defense cannot be reconciled with the *words* of the statute, but only with its *purpose*" (at p. 13, above), and argues that the same purpose that supports self-defense supports the present sort of killing. The trouble with these arguments is that they license judges to speculate on the purposes of our laws and to draw conclusions from their speculations. There is no quicker way to unleash judges from the law and turn them loose to follow their personal opinions. The true reason why self-defense is a recognized exception to the murder statute, when the statute contains no words to recognize it, is that it was so recognized by all legislators, judges, and citizens at the time the statute was framed and adopted. It was no part of the original legislative intent to alter such an ancient and universal rule; if it were, the legislature knew how to make its desire unmistakable. Similarly, we need no tortured argument about willfulness to show that capital punishment is compatible with our murder statute; it is compatible because, like self-defense, it was lawful and commonplace at the time our statute was adopted.

We have heard that the murder statute makes an exception for human instinct, or that necessity negates willfulness. When my colleagues make assertions of this kind about what our statute means, I'm sure they think they are speaking sensibly. But I do not know how a statute can mean anything other than what its words commonly mean to ordinary speakers of that language. If ordinary speakers disagree on what certain words mean, then we might ask what the author of those words meant by them. But we do not ask judges as if they were a distinct and independent authority on meaning.

The plain meaning of the words in our murder statute does not support any speculation about an exception for human instinct or the exculpatory effect of necessity. And I am quite sure that the legislators who drafted and adopted that statute, and the executive who signed it into law, never had such legal niceties in their minds. Self-defense and lawful execution, by contrast, were without doubt in the minds of them all.

The legislative branch of government deserves our respect, but not always our admiration. All too rarely does it contain a soul with any detailed knowledge or deep concern about the criminal law and its underlying moral questions. The non-lawyers in the legislature surely never trouble themselves with human instinct, necessity, or *mens rea*. The lawyers there are mostly practitioners of civil and corporate law, whose fortunes have enabled them to run successfully for office; their knowledge of criminal law is limited to the one course they were forced to take in law school. The few with criminal law training are usually prosecutors whose fame in prosecuting corrupt politicians catapulted them into the legislature. Their professional interest in criminal law is to find strategies to put targeted defendants behind bars, not to think deeply about the moral principles that underlie, or ought to underlie, our methods for ascertaining criminal responsibility. As prosecutors, they had no need to justify the willfulness requirement in the murder statute or to explain its rationale; they had only to persuade a jury that an evildoer was willful. Moreover, even those with some reflective concern about the principles of our criminal law are asked to vote for, or against, an omnibus crime bill of stupendous size, far too long for any but "jailhouse lawyers" to read in its entirety. And at least half of these votes are extracted by party leadership, pressured by lobbyist inducements, or traded for reciprocating votes from other legislators on other bills, and need not reflect the legislator's own views, if indeed the legislator has views on the bill. In short, the original intent of this statute is nothing nearly as sophisticated as my colleagues have made out. On the contrary, the non-specialists who happened to have a vote on legislation were probably told by the specialists on their staffs that the word "willful" was a good idea in the statute to sort out the kinds of killers we wish to punish from those we do not.

Moreover, of course, even if all legislators understood the language on which they voted, and had conscientious views on its underlying policies and principles

– and voted by their consciences – their divisions and disagreements prevent us from saying that "the legislature" had any single intent. And even if it acted unanimously, should we also consult the intent of every subsequent legislature that had the power to revise or repeal the statute but chose not to do so?

These arguments lead us to follow the plain meaning of words like "willful" rather than the most recent, most sophisticated theory to be found in our academic law journals. If anyone should point out that the original intent of the legislature and the plain meaning of its words might conflict, I will concede the point at once. But the alternative cannot be to put legislative intent and plain meaning aside in favor of the visions most appealing to the personal tastes or moral opinions of a judge.

I have argued that moral principles underlie the law, but at the same time I have argued that judges should regard law and morality as independent. If I have been overly concise, then one qualification should make the compatibility of these claims clear: law and morality are inseparable for the legislature, independent for the judiciary. The legislature has moral motives when it prohibits murder; it thinks murder is wrong and prohibits it because it is wrong. No one doubts this or wants it any other way. Judges, however, hold no license from the people to enforce their own moral views. Their job is to interpret the words of the legislature, which reflect the moral views of the legislature, which reflect something like the moral views of the people.

We interpret the words of a statute according to their plain meaning, as ordinary citizens and jurors might understand them, and resolve difficulties in light of historical practices at the time the statute was adopted, including the intent of its authors if that is clearly known. This is the only recipe human beings have ever found for constraining themselves to apply law, and to avoid exercising a despotic power beyond law.

V

I remind my brethren of three excellent reasons not to overrule law in the name of morality or to blend law and morality in the name of interpretation. The first is that we are appointed for life. Hence we are entirely insulated from the political process; we are not accountable to the people. Hence we should be the last officials in this government to make decisions based on policy or any of its tempting surrogates, such as morality or justice. The only reason we are insulated from the political process is to allow us to follow the law when that proves politically difficult. Because the legally easy verdict in this case is politically difficult to pronounce, it could not be a clearer call to duty for us.

The second reason is that when previous justices of this Court showed an insolent tendency to make judgments in which personal views of morality displaced or diluted the law of the land, the people rebelled (Keen at p. 21, above). The ensuing civil war devastated the Commonwealth by its many atrocities on both sides; we will never regain our innocence. Even if the proper role of a judge was unclear before the civil war, it should be very clear now.

The third reason is that we live in a pluralistic society. Those who ask us to put the law aside in the name of justice evidently assume that our private notions of justice agree with theirs. If we made it a rule to put the law aside to enforce our private notions of justice, then we would offend and oppress all those citizens whose moral opinions differed from our own. There might even be some excuse for this in a homogeneous society in which law itself differed little from popular morality, and those offended by judicial legislation were the same as those offended by legislative legislation. But we live in a pluralistic society. This means that our disagreements on moral questions are real, not merely apparent, and are deep, not superficial. It also means that we have reached a meta-level agreement that no one of these many contending views is privileged over the others for the purposes of law and government. One of these views may temporarily dominate our political life if its proponents become a numerical majority and use the ballot box intelligently. But, again, we have reached a meta-level agreement that in principle every numerical minority may become a numerical majority. So though we elect legislators by counting votes, we do not give citizens with "morally superior" views more than one vote. To live in a pluralistic society means that no view may for any official purpose be regarded as morally superior to any other. But if this is so, I could only put the law aside in the name of justice if I were willing to tyrannize over those who differed from me on the requirements of justice. If the people as a whole speak through the law, then to put the law aside in the name of justice is to thwart the people in the name of the favored sub-group that thinks like the judge. In that sense, appeals to justice beyond law are elitist attempts to subvert democracy, and are most dangerous when we are most tempted to agree with them. As long as we take pains to let all views be heard in the law-making process, which we do, then the only way to preserve peace and tranquillity, even justice, in a pluralistic society is to uphold the law, and never to put it aside in favor of moral or political views endorsed by only one faction, sect, or bloc.

In the absence of these three reasons, one would act well and wisely to favor the morally compelling verdict over the legally compelling verdict when the two differed. But these three reasons force the opposite conclusion. An old joke among our law students has it that if you wish to study justice, you ought quit the Law School and register in the Philosophy Department or Divinity School. This is supposed to be funny, I suppose, or to put our profession in a bad light. I never understood it that way. Law differs from ideal justice in many things, but one point of difference is that law reflects the vision of ideal justice that a particular people at a particular time has agreed shall govern them, and to secure this agreement many compromises from each person's private ideal must be accepted.

But to those morally impatient idealists who misunderstand the place of law in human affairs, who seek justice above and beyond the law, and who place their own visions of justice above the compromises produced by the democratic process, I may add, finally, that law itself contains a solution to the problem. The purpose of executive clemency (in John Locke's words) is to mitigate the rigors of the law. If our law is clear but unduly harsh, then judges ought to do what the law clearly requires, because it is the law, and the executive ought to consider clemency because the law is unduly harsh. Obviously, to say this is not at all to shift responsibility to the executive in the way that Justice Foster criticized Justice Truepenny for proposing (at p. 10, above). On the contrary, it is a way of taking responsibility as a judge for a verdict that is required by law regardless of its harshness.

I vote to uphold the conviction.

OPINION OF JUSTICE
SPRINGHAM

I

Nothing in the opinions of *Spelunkers I* surprises me except the insistence that this case is simple. Justices Truepenny and Keen believe it obvious that the four original defendants willfully killed Roger Whetmore. In the present case Justice Burnham agrees as to the fifth defendant. Foster and Handy appeal to different grounds to acquit the men but agree that acquittal is the only obvious course for a court of law. What is obvious to me is that this is a hard case. Justice Tatting understood that, but couldn't live up to his understanding. Hard cases have answers, just as easy ones do, although they impose greater duties of care and scrupulosity on judges and do not guarantee that conscientious judges will agree. They are not excuses to appeal to one's private moral convictions, as Foster and Handy do in the end. They are not excuses to shut one's eyes to the complexity of law that makes one's oath of office difficult to fulfill, as Truepenny and Keen do in the end. They are not excuses to oversimplify the relationship between law and morality, as Burnham does. Nor are they excuses to find a tie and give up, as Tatting does.

Under the laws of the state of Newgarth, the spelunkers committed no murder. Hence I vote to overturn the conviction of the defendant. I emphasize that he is not acquitted by abstract justice, reason, common sense, natural law, popular morality, or opinion polls, but by the positive law of Newgarth, particularly the statute defining murder and the precedents interpreting it.

I detect in the opinions of my colleagues an oversimple opposition between cases in which judgment is forced (because the law is clear) and cases in which discretion is necessary or extra-legal considerations permissible (because the law is not clear). However, when I say that this is above all a hard case, I do not mean to permit appeal to discretion or extra-legal considerations.

I am encouraged that, to a person, the justices in *Spelunkers I* did not think they were free to use discretion. Truepenny and Keen uphold the conviction with regret; if they thought they had discretion, presumably they would have decided the other way. In the present case, Burnham takes a similar stand. If Tatting thought he had discretion, he could easily have found a personal basis for tilting the balance that he could not tilt in any other way. Foster uses two ingenious arguments and Handy appeals to public opinion; even if they are mistaken, these are standards rather than free uses of discretion. Because we are not free to use our discretion, we must investigate what the law requires. Because this is a hard case, we expect that this investigation will in turn be hard, perhaps Herculean; hence we must be resolute in respecting the complexity of law and sensitive to the slightest nuances of principle.

II

The defendant was convicted of murder, so we must begin with the murder statute. It requires us to punish him if he killed willfully. He admits that he participated with his four comrades in the killing of Roger Whetmore. The only question, then, is whether they killed him willfully.

One reason that this is a hard case is that these facts prevent us from reaching a stable conclusion using our customary notions of willfulness. The spelunkers clearly planned to kill someone. They spent a good deal of time discussing the mathematics of their lottery. The point of the lottery was to select a victim to kill. They did not select Whetmore deliberately, but they did employ a lottery deliberately, and they did intend to kill the person it selected. Whetmore was not selected or killed by a bolt of lightning. His comrades killed him intentionally, not accidentally. They killed as the result of a prior plan, not provocation or blind impulse. They did not even attempt an insanity defense at trial. And as Burnham points out, they did not claim that Whetmore died of natural causes or accident before they could kill him. All this argues in favor of finding willfulness.

But they had no ill-will. While they did not kill from a blind impulse, they did kill from the motive of self-preservation. Justice Tatting notes that killing in self-defense is not willful in the legal sense of the term because it proceeds from an impulse of self-preservation that is "deeply ingrained" in our nature (at p. 17, above). If calm, open-eyed self-defense is not willful, then this act is not willful; we can agree on this even if we do not consider this to be a case of self-defense (and I do not). Similarly, while these men chose to kill, they could not have chosen otherwise without choosing death for themselves. They had no reasonable options; that is what we mean when we say they found themselves in dire or exigent circumstances. It is what we mean when we say they killed from "necessity" (which I will explore below). All this argues against finding willfulness.

Normally the intention to kill implies the existence of other more reasonable options that the law requires one to choose instead of killing. Normally premeditation implies evil will. Normally lack of impulse implies culpable clarity of mind. But this killing upsets all these expectations. The many senses of the word "willful" divide on these facts. These men acted from premeditation and intention; but they did not act from ill-will, and they lacked *mens rea* for the same reason that self-defenders do.

If the word "willful" supports and subverts both sides in this case, it does not follow that the word "willful" is useless as a standard for our decision. Nor does it follow that law has here *come to an end* like a trail of breadcrumbs in the forest, and that we must proceed from this point without guidance from law. We cannot decide whatever we please. We may subjectively be torn by conflicting principles and feel deep uncertainty. But we have no grounds to believe that our subjective uncertainty reflects an objective indeterminacy of the law, and hence no grounds to surrender to the difficulties of this case by appeal to unfettered discretion, "self-evident justice" or "the spirit of the law" beyond the letter.

The proper way to decide whether this killing was willful *in the relevant sense* is to examine the other cases of this Court in which the word "willful" was interpreted. For example, if mercy killing is willful, then premeditation would seem to count for more than lack of ill-will. If a tire manufacturer is found "willful" in the death of a person in an automobile accident caused by a defective tire it knowingly sold, then the availability of reasonable alternative courses of conduct would seem to count for more than the absence of impulse. And so on. But unfortunately, the precedents on this point are unavailable to us.*

Since we presume innocence until guilt is proved, and require guilt in a criminal case to be proved beyond a reasonable doubt, we should resolve all these doubts in favor of the defendant. This unimpeachable rule of procedure requires that we acquit the defendant. But suppose this rule never existed.

III

Another way to resolve these doubts that is more satisfactory, because it requires us to look closely at the law of our Commonwealth, is to consider that the word

---

*   The members of the Supreme Court were obliged to write their opinions in the present case during the so-called "product recall" of Nomos Information Systems. Nomos publishes the statutes and cases of our Commonwealth in electronic form, and has done so with such success that it has driven all rivals from the field. Indeed, the Commonwealth Publishing Office stopped publishing its own version of our laws nearly half a century ago in a short-sighted move to reduce the costs of government. Nomos is now engaged in litigation with a group of professional legal associations who seek to open the electronic files of our law to the public without charge. Nomos claims a copyright on its version of the laws, based on its pagination scheme and the scholarly apparatus it has mixed with the texts. To exert pressure in the long-running settlement talks, Nomos has taken its files offline. While no one should believe that the Commonwealth has accepted this impediment to justice with acquiescence, pressure from the three branches of government has so far been unavailing. Consequently, for the time being, not even the Supreme Court has access to most of the cases decided in the last fifty years.

In *Commonwealth v. Runes*, decided shortly after the recall began, we held (1) that the courts of Newgarth, including this Court, cannot cease to decide cases during the product recall, and (2) that it would be improper for any court, including this Court, to cite cases for which it has no authoritative text. This dilemma will require different solutions in different cases. *Runes* itself, like the other cases decided since the recall began, is available for citation because we still have the text in hand.

"willful" in the murder statute functions to express the requirement of *mens rea* or "guilty mind." Without it we would punish every person who caused the death of another, regardless of the defendant's state of mind at the time; we would never distinguish murder from other homicides. The *mens rea* requirement forces us to acquit those who lack the requisite mental state – for example, young children, the severely retarded, the temporarily insane, and those otherwise competent adults who are under the temporary sway of passion, provocation, or special kinds of ignorance or mistake. If we could look at the history of Newgarth precedents interpreting the word "willful" we would not find dictionary definitions aimed at capturing the usage of the speakers of our language, or historical excavations of our legislative proceedings aimed at capturing the intent of our long-dead legislators, but legal definitions aimed at capturing the principle or concept of *mens rea*.

In the absence of those precedents we are no worse off than we would be if those precedents were inconsistent. And we often find ourselves in such an adjudicative impasse. Facing such an obstacle, adjudication returns to its roots in moral and political philosophy. The word "willful" does not designate what our historical legislators actually had in their minds at the time they voted on the statute, let alone what the lay person on the streets of New York imagines the word to mean, as Burnham suggests. Burnham shows well, though perhaps unintentionally, what a morass of confusion would underlie our law if those divergent and jumbled thoughts were to replace, or even supplement, our canons of interpretation. Instead, the word "willful" designates the *concept of willfulness*. Our job is to interpret that concept, acknowledging that we can do no better than to approach it through our own individual conceptions. But there is no other way. Even the "plain meaning" of the word invites us to meditate on that concept, not to unearth the diaries of our ancestors or poll the citizens on the street.

Burnham's fear that this exercise frees judges from the fetters of law is so palpably misguided that one suspects it is facetious. Our job is to interpret the concept designated by the legislature, a strong and public constraint; our job is not to interpret our own preferences or to replace the legislature's concept with one we like better. This is the very opposite of license or discretion.

Newgarth recognizes necessity as a general defense to criminal charges. This is clear both from *Staymore* and the ancient, nameless precedent that first recognized the exception for self-defense. Both the murder statute and the parking ordinance in *Staymore* are silent on the necessity defense, and indeed taken literally exclude this defense. We may go further: Newgarth has no statutory necessity defense. But this fact does not imply that the necessity defense is not recognized in our law or is incompatible with the moral principles of our civilization; and it certainly has not stopped our courts from acquitting defendants on the grounds of necessity, with the acceptance of the community. Those cases now comprise precedents under which we must interpret the word "willful" and the silence of the murder statute on excuses and justifications.

The legal principle embodied in the necessity defense is that people who commit crimes from necessity lack *mens rea* or criminal intent and should not be punished. The question of willfulness, then, reduces to the question of necessity. If the spelunkers killed from necessity, then they lacked criminal intent, or did not kill willfully in the relevant sense, and should be acquitted.

Moreover, the spelunkers did kill from necessity. The alternative was to die, which is the strongest kind of necessity.

Justice Burnham has usefully compiled six objections to the claim of necessity here (at pp. 38f, above), although he capitulates to them far too quickly. Let us consider these six objections in order.

1. Were the spelunkers sure they would die? To put this in other terms, was their belief in necessity a reasonable belief in the circumstances? Burnham is right that good faith belief in necessity, without reasonableness, is not enough; for then we would live in a crank's anarchy, at the mercy of the false, foolish, and unfounded but still sincere beliefs in the necessity of violating criminal laws held by every lunatic. Since the necessity defense puts us at risk of losing the rule of law, we must examine closely the reasonableness of the belief in its existence.

The answer is fortunately clear in this case. The spelunkers had already been imprisoned in their cave for twenty days when finally reached by radio. They had expert opinion from the engineers supervising the rescue that they could not be freed for at least ten more days. They had expert opinion from physicians on the scene that there was "little possibility" that they could live ten additional days without food (see p. 8, above). They had expert opinion from the same physicians that they could live at least ten days longer if they ate one of their companions (see p. 8, above). They asked for expert legal and moral opinion on the possibility of killing a member of their party for food, and were given nothing but silence. It is offensive to second-guess the actions of starving men trapped under the earth. But in this case it is crystal clear that their belief in the necessity of desperate action was reasonable in the circumstances. It was grounded not in self-serving predictions of their longevity, clouded by weakness and panic; it was grounded in expert opinion. Indeed, it is difficult to imagine a case in which men might be forced to kill and eat a companion on better information.

Justice Burnham points out that Whetmore was willing to wait another week. This is true but does not mean that Whetmore's opinion was true, that it was more reasonable than the opinions of his killers, or even that it was reasonable at all. His hesitation could well be explained by queasiness and fear. The spelunkers had to choose whether to believe Whetmore or the engineers and doctors on the radio. Given that choice, they acted most reasonably.

2. Despite the strong case for necessity, the prosecution objects that *Valjean* means that starvation is not a legally recognized kind of necessity. We reject this reading. In *Valjean*, a man stole a loaf of bread from hunger, pleaded necessity, and was convicted. There are many grounds for distinguishing *Valjean* from the facts of our case. First, Valjean might not have been starving. We don't know the extremity of his hunger; therefore we don't know the extremity of his necessity. Second, even if Valjean were starving, he did not have the same expert opinion

to support his belief in necessity. The spelunkers had much better proof of these crucial facts. Third, Valjean had several options open to him other than crime. We will not insult his desperation by telling him he could have found a job. However, begging is not against the laws of Newgarth. Many churches and secular charities feed the poor. Demeaning as he might have found these remedies, they were freely available to him. The spelunkers in the cave did not have options nearly as attractive open to them. So we read *Valjean* to deny the necessity defense to a man with enough options available to him to negate his claim of necessity; it does not deny the existence of the necessity defense *per se* or deny that starvation could count as necessity.

3. The prosecution argues further that the spelunkers may have had fewer attractive options than Jean Valjean, but they had more than one. As long as no one of them was volunteering to commit suicide, they could have eaten their own fingers and toes, for example. They could also have waited for the first of them to die of starvation. This is clearly a painful course, but it would allow them to avoid murder. They would all be very much weakened by the time the first of them died, unless one were very much weaker than the others from the start. But their inability to "dig in" or take energetic advantage of the first natural death among them is not an argument. They had an obligation to try everything short of killing before they tried killing, especially if they are to claim that they killed "from necessity."

This argument is strong but it can be answered. If the spelunkers reasonably believed that they would be rescued at any time, then they should have begun with "snacks" and "feasted" only when their snacks ran out. But they had expert opinion that they could not be rescued for at least ten days. It is not reasonable to believe that an already starving man could live ten days on the nutritional equivalent of a dessert plate of ladies' fingers. In light of their expert information, they would have had to eat something more substantial like arms or legs. But again, why not? Is that not better than to kill? Here we begin second-guessing the wisdom of men whose desperate situation we can scarcely imagine. Would it be better to die or to be tortured for a week or more by having a limb or two gnawed off without anaesthetic? The same question applies to torture in the form of death by starvation. Here the benefit of the doubt belongs to the men who were left to choose their method of suffering.

The objection raises the problem of proportionality. We say that killing in self-defense, for example, is killing from necessity and hence justified. But the killing must be proportional to the harm threatened, or to the harm one reasonably believes to be threatened. So one may not kill a bully who kicks sand in one's face, or a rival at checkers who is about to win. But at the edge, when it is unclear whether death is threatened, we give the benefit of the doubt to the self-defender, as here we must give it to the self-preserver. So, for example, one may kill a maniac who is punching one with his fists. One may kill an unknown person climbing into one's bedroom window at night even without waiting for the general threat to become more specific. Much more may be reasonable to the person in peril than is reasonable to the prosecutor using hindsight. Our standard is to ask whether the defendant had a reasonable belief in the necessity. This requires us to use his own standpoint, as vicarious as it is for us and as unimaginative as we may be.

We admit the proportionality requirement on the necessity defense, of course. But we deny that it requires these spelunkers to humor the prosecution with ineffectual snacks or to suffer torture before facing the necessity to kill. Even the proportionality requirement in cases of self-defense gives the benefit of the doubt to the person in peril and refuses to judge the reasonableness of his belief by the standards of calm, well-fed, well-protected, long-thinking persons who are secure in the warm arms of civilization and are exercising hindsight.

4. Again, the prosecution argues that the necessity defense is not available to those for whom the necessity arises as the result of their own choice or negligence. Otherwise we would have to acquit the cunning cannibal who intentionally locks himself and a hapless captive in an abandoned bank vault unknown to the rest of the world, waits until they are hungry, and then kills his companion for food. These men knew that spelunking was a risky sport. They took a radio; they told the secretary of their society where and when they planned to emerge from the cave so that a rescue could be commenced if they were trapped. They assumed the risk of their adventure willingly. Indeed, facing risk is part of the exhilaration of the sport. When they lose their gamble, can they use their misfortune to excuse their crime?

I answer that they did not choose to be buried in a landslide; nor did they become buried through their own negligence. They did indeed pursue a risky sport from free choice. But that does not mean the necessity of their ultimate condition can be traced to their choice or negligence. If we thought otherwise, we would have to deny the necessity defense to those who destroy private property, like the windows belonging to their landlord, when escaping from a burning house, on the ground that they "assumed the risk" of living in a wooden building. The absurdity of such an argument shows that we may take many risks without forfeiting a necessity defense when the predicament we risked unhappily materializes.

But shouldn't we deny the necessity defense to *these* men whose risk was *especially* remote from routine risks of life and travel? This argument would be stronger if the men knowingly entered a cave susceptible to an imminent landslide, or if the thrill of surviving a landslide were one of the excitements they craved as sportsmen. But there is no evidence to support these conjectures.

5. The prosecution can shift the objection. The men could have taken extra provisions. That does not make them negligent in becoming buried by a landslide, but it does make them negligent in becoming pinched by the necessity to kill a companion for food. They were not negligent in pursuing a risky sport, but in doing so with insufficient provisions.

This argument is attractive at first glance, but its weakness is soon apparent. What if the men had taken ever so many provisions? It is still possible that the extent of the landslide or difficulty of the rescue could have outflanked their foresight. No matter how careful they were, hence no matter how little they were negligent, we can still imagine that the necessity of killing a companion for food could arise.

Did these men bring a *reasonable* amount of extra food to face the risks they freely assumed? I think so. They had enough to allow six men to survive twenty-three days after the landslide and an unknown time before the landslide. We do not know how long they planned to live on their provisions, but they did live on them for twenty-three days longer than they planned to. Those who have carried food on their backs into the wilderness know that twenty-three days' worth is barely hoistable. In the absence of reliable facts as to their original plans, we must find their provisions adequate to acquit them of negligence.

Here I must pause to consider an insidious tendency in Justice Burnham's arguments. What if the spelunkers had taken six months' worth of food beyond their planned needs, simply as insurance against a landslide? Burnham would use that fact to argue that they had "assumed the risk" of a landslide. He used the spelunkers' other precautions against them in just this way, inferring assumption of risk from the fact that they carried a radio and arranged for the secretary of their society to initiate a rescue if they did not return by a certain date.

Burnham cannot have it both ways. If the spelunkers had *not* carried a radio, or had *not* arranged with the secretary of their society to be rescued, he would be the first to accuse them of negligence, and the first to use it against them in denying their necessity defense. But if those who take precautions assume the risk, and those who take no precautions are negligent, then nobody deserves a necessity defense. This is Burnham's argument in a nutshell. Nobody deserves a necessity defense. The plain meaning of the statute excludes it, and our unsophisticated legislators never dreamt of it; there is no necessity defense. This radical position underlies all his bluster about the rule of law standing in jeopardy. His argument, however, is more convenient than persuasive; for as he well knows, from *Staymore*, which he cites himself, the case law of our Commonwealth does recognize a necessity defense. Moreover, cases upholding the necessity defense in various branches of law were routinely decided at the time of the adoption of our murder statute, to use a criterion close to Burnham's heart.

6. Even if these men were under a true necessity to kill, the objection goes, their method of selecting Whetmore to die was unfair. Whetmore consented to hold a lottery but then revoked his consent. He acquiesced in the fairness of his toss of the dice, but not to the fairness of selecting anyone by lot to die. So in the last analysis he was coerced, just like the victim of a street murder.

Or so Justice Burnham argues. But if a random lottery is a fair method to select a victim (assuming it is necessary to select a victim), then the victim's consent is irrelevant. This fact dispels great clouds of confusion that have dimmed the vision of my colleagues. They worry whether the spelunkers' several consents to the pact gave the pact legal standing. They worry that Whetmore's revocation of consent before his dice throw might have nullified the pact. They wonder whether his consent to the fairness of the dice throw made on his behalf implies a consent to rejoin the compact and be killed if he loses the throw.

All this discussion is irrelevant because, as a matter of law, the consent of the victim is not a defense to murder in Newgarth. Our murder statute makes the state of mind of the killer decisive, that of the victim irrelevant. Therefore, even had all members consented and persisted in their consent, the pact could never have justified a murder. The revocation of consent was as irrelevant as the original consent.

If the spelunkers were justified by necessity, then they do not need additional justification, such as consent of the victim. They certainly do not need such additional justification when it amounts to no justification at all under our laws. So these spelunkers were justified by necessity, not by consent. The victim was selected fairly because the method was random, not because the method was consensual.

Whether the defendant acted from necessity, and whether his belief in necessity was reasonable in the circumstances, are questions of fact. These questions were considered by the jury at trial, and we are bound to give the jury findings great deference. As an appellate court we review questions of law and are ill-equipped to initiate a fresh inquiry into the facts. However, we must hold the findings of the jury to the standard of proof in criminal cases. The defendant must be proved guilty beyond a reasonable doubt or else acquitted. In this case the grounds for the necessity defense are overwhelming. Therefore we must reverse the jury on this point. Even if the case for necessity were not overwhelming, we must conclude that the case against it is not overwhelming, as it would have to be to justify conviction beyond a reasonable doubt.

This conclusion provides an easy answer to Justice Burnham's ingenious but disingenuous example of the moneyed murderer with intent but no ill-will. Burnham says there is no legally relevant difference between that hypothetical killing and the present actual one. But this is simply false, for the sartorial psychopath undoubtedly did not kill from necessity and the spelunkers undoubtedly did so.

In short, the defendant acted from necessity. His belief in the necessity of his act was reasonable. Necessity negates the *mens rea* requirement of our criminal law expressed in our murder statute by the word "willful." Therefore the defendant did not kill willfully. Therefore he did not violate the statute under which he was convicted. Therefore his conviction must be overturned.

IV

But suppose that all the preceding argument is mistaken. Suppose that the necessity defense were not recognized in Newgarth at all, *Staymore* and the ancient recognition of self-defense notwithstanding. Or suppose that our case law interpreting the word "willful" were suddenly available again, and shown to compel the conclusion that the spelunkers did act willfully.

We know from *Fehler* that the literal meaning of a statute can be overridden by the legislative intent, at least when the latter is clear. In *Fehler* a typographical error in the statute book did not stop this Court from reading the statute in light of its intended meaning, disregarding its absurd literal meaning.

As Justice Burnham points out, the purpose of our murder statute is not as clear as that of the misprinted statute in *Fehler*. Under *Parry* the purpose of the murder statute is to deter future murders. Under *Makeover* it is to justify coercive rehabilitation of those dangerous fellow citizens who have not learned to control their behavior. Under *Scape* it is to provide an orderly outlet for the natural human demand for retribution.

Justice Burnham infers from the plurality of these theories that we must not look for the purpose of our murder statute. But he should have looked instead at their content. For it does not matter which of these readings we favor; *none* justifies us in punishing the defendant. Punishing him will not deter anyone so unfortunate as to be trapped in the same circumstances in the future. We admit this as soon as we acknowledge that he acted from necessity. Punishing him will not deter and (if we are honest in drawing the lesson from the necessity defense) *ought not* to deter anyone similarly situated. For the same reason, the defendant does not require rehabilitation. He did nothing to betray a bad character requiring correction for the safety of the public or himself. On the contrary, he and his comrades acted with exemplary restraint and reasonableness in a situation under which most of the rest of us would have folded from frailty and fright. Even Burnham admits that most good people would do what these men did if they possessed the same courage and found themselves in the same circumstances. Finally, while there is a natural demand for retribution in most killings, it is well known that there is none in this case. To recognize that fact is not at all to let popular opinion displace the law. It is to observe that the ancient purpose of satisfying a deep-seated and instinctual demand for vengeance, or to prevent the self-help likely when this demand is not satisfied, does not apply in this case.

In short, however we read the purpose of this statute, that purpose will not be served by punishing this defendant. So even if he is guilty under the statute (which he is not), the statute should be suspended on the ground that applying it here serves no end of the law. To punish this defendant would put abstract form ahead of substance.

V

These arguments are sufficient to acquit the defendant and independent of each other, so that if one is rejected the other will do the job alone. It would distract us from the strength and sufficiency of these arguments to offer additional, but weaker, arguments, simply in the spirit of multiplying arguments.

So I make no appeal to the claim of Justice Foster that the statutes of Newgarth do not apply to the spelunkers because they existed in a state of nature. However, Foster had two arguments ostensibly about the state of nature that contain a kernel of truth prematurely rejected by my colleagues.

It is true, as Foster reminds us (at p. 10, above), that *cessante ratione legis, cessat et ipsa lex* (where the reason for the law ceases, the law itself ceases). This is a principle of statutory construction as well as of justice. It is by no means the supernatural or superstitious appeal to natural law that Tatting suggests it is (at p. 16, above) or that Foster unfortunately intimates it might be (at p. 10, above). However, this is to say that Foster's state-of-nature argument, when properly expressed, reduces to the argument already stated, that no purpose of the law is served by punishing these spelunkers.

Similarly, Justice Foster argued that, once trapped, the spelunkers lived in a state of nature, therefore beyond our legal authority, even though they still lived within our territorial boundaries. This is an unfortunate way to express an argument with a kernel of truth – unfortunate for suggesting that the jurisdiction of a court is like a gas seeping from the courtroom, obeying physical laws, stopped in its spread by tons of rock rather than by our human conventions and agreements. The kernel of truth in Foster's argument was alluded to by Foster himself when he recited the familiar facts that the state of Newgarth was founded upon an explicit contract by the survivors of the holocaust during the first period following the Great Spiral (at p. 12, above). As John Locke had said millennia before, a local and temporary state of war may arise within a state of law whenever a man threatens another's life; and a local and temporary state of nature may arise within a state of law whenever the purposes of the social contract are locally suspended.

Foster's argument does not deny that a state of law existed before, during, and after the landslide that trapped the spelunkers. Properly understood, it does not assert that the thickness of the rock or the difficulty of the rescue put them beyond our laws. Instead it reminds us that our laws are based on a contract entered for certain purposes. When those purposes are impossible to meet because of tragic but contingent circumstances, the obligations of the contract are also suspended, just as my contractual promise to paint your house is suspended when your house burns down. We recognized this in *Staymore*, in which the defendant was physically unable to move his car from its parking place because of an unforeseen political demonstration. His obligation to stay in that parking place no more than two hours was released by the fact that the reciprocal obligations running to him under the social contract had been suspended by events beyond his control.

The kernel of truth in Foster's argument, in short, is captured by the necessity defense. He invited the misunderstanding and ridicule he received from Justice Tatting. But my colleagues must acknowledge that, if they reject Foster's argument, and assert in its place that we have obligations that transcend our circumstances and conventions, then they undercut the necessity defense we recognized in *Staymore*, they undercut our ancient recognition of self-defense, and they undercut as well the legitimacy of our government in a contract.

VI

Finally, let us suppose that all the arguments above are mistaken. The defendant is guilty as charged. There is still a good reason in Newgarth law to spare his life. If the defendant is guilty as charged, then it is because the necessity of his act was deemed irrelevant. But any statute that makes mitigating circumstances irrelevant is *prima facie* a violation of the defendant's right to fundamental fairness, or what we formerly called due process of law. This is especially true when the statute stipulates a mandatory death penalty, as in the present case. When the stakes are this high, then we must in justice consider any mitigating circumstances the defense may offer. Similarly, when only one punishment is allowed by law, judges are denied the flexibility to make the punishment fit the crime. It is certainly true that the legislature intended to deny this flexibility to the judiciary. However, it is equally certain that the legislature, without insulation from the political process provided to the judiciary, can be carried by passion and political temptation far beyond the bounds of the constitution and the dictates of fundamental fairness.

Even if our earlier arguments were unavailing, then, we would have to nullify that part of the murder statute that makes death the one and only penalty for all murderers, regardless of the profound differences among them, their states of mind, and the circumstances of their actions. Even if guilty, the defendant need not die. After nullifying that part of the murder statute, we would remand the case to the trial court for sentencing.

I vote to overturn the conviction.

OPINION OF JUSTICE TALLY

I

We all acknowledge that killing in self-defense is not murder in Newgarth, and that killing in self-defense is entirely justified. Like most of my colleagues, I do not consider this to be a case of self-defense; but, unlike most of my colleagues, I find illumination for the present case in the exercise of meditating on our venerable rule to acquit intentional killers when we find that they killed in self-defense. The result of this meditation is additional support for the conclusion already argued in detail by Justice Springham that this killing is not murder because it was necessary. I write a separate opinion chiefly because I find that he misunderstood the nature of the necessity defense.

The fact we acquit those who kill in self-defense signifies that killing *per se* is not the wrong we seek to punish through our murder statute. And because killing in self-defense can be intentional, not even intentional killing *per se* is the wrong we seek to punish.

When a defendant claims that he killed in self-defense, we examine the claim to see whether some lesser exertion of force might have sufficed to protect his life. In some circumstances we ask whether he might have retreated or fled to avoid the conflict altogether. But if we find that retreat was impossible, unsafe, or unnecessary, and that fatal force was the only degree that would give a reasonable assurance of self-protection, and that the defendant was not the aggressor in the affray that led to his fatal exercise of self-defense, then we acquit. Having found these elements, we do not ask whether the defendant found himself in his predicament through his own negligence, or through some foolish or sporting risk shunned by most citizens. We do not expect him to have waited for police if we know, but he did not know and could not reasonably have known, that he was within minutes of a police rescue. We do not ask whether he might have haggled or delayed to gain the consent of his victim, or blame him for proceeding without that consent.

By accepting self-defense, we accept the killing of A to prevent the killing of B, which might be called *preventive killing*. Now here is a hard question: why do we ever tolerate preventive killing?

One reason we tolerate preventive killing in the case of self-defense is that we judge that in those unfortunate circumstances someone has to die and that it is better for the aggressor to die than for the innocent victim of aggression to die. This is why the present case is not one of self-defense; Whetmore was not an aggressor or any less worthy of life than his comrades. He was as innocent as his fellow spelunkers, and the intentional killing of an innocent cannot be justified by self-defense. These men were truly forced to take drastic steps to live; but this was not the fault of Whetmore. This is also why we would not accept a plea of self-defense from a convicted murderer who managed to kill his guards and executioner just as he was about to be executed; for in that situation, it is better for *him* to die than for *them* to die.

Another reason why we accept preventive killing, I submit, is that we value life. In particular, we value life in such a way that we would always prefer that *more* people survive a tragic accident than *fewer*. My colleagues are remarkably shy about saying what I presume they all believe, which is that killing one person in order to save five *is a bargain*. It is horrible for such a step to be necessary. But clearly it is better that one should die, enabling five to survive, *than that all six should die*. Only the most radical religious fanatics dissent from this view.

I suspect that some of my colleagues assent to the argument here in principle, but find that their intuition balks at its application to the present case. But let us suppose instead that one man were killed in order to prevent the deaths of *one million* people. This is a very significant change, at least for most people's intuitions. At these numbers we would undoubtedly have volunteers to sacrifice themselves for the sake of the million in need. But again, suppose we had none and had to resort to a fair lottery. If one million to one is an acceptable ratio, which justifies killing a non-volunteer when no other relief is possible, then why not five to one? The principle is the same. Are we really prepared to quibble about the ratio? If five to one is too low a ratio, too poor a bargain, then when does it become *sufficiently* high? Such casuistry is demeaning to the Court, impossible in practice, and unnecessary to decide this case. The principle of the greater good means that the exact ratio is irrelevant, provided that a greater number of people gained than lost.

On this view, the state of Newgarth is justified in demanding the death penalty for murderers in order to prevent them from killing again. That is, the state is justified in killing murderers when it is a "bargain" in the technical sense to do so. Similarly, Newgarth would be justified in going to war to repel an aggressor whenever it is justified in thinking that killing a large number of enemy soldiers would prevent the deaths of an even greater number of other people. I do not know whether Newgarth does execute murderers and go to war in the name of this principle – and I agree with Justice Burnham that it is folly to speculate, for long, on the real purposes of our laws. This is only to show that the principle, far from being cold-hearted and alien, may justify some of our most familiar and venerable moral practices.

The ten workmen killed in the rescue were victims of regrettable accidents.

No one thought then, and no one thinks now, that purchasing the lives of the six spelunkers at the cost of the ten workmen would be a bargain. The workmen were not intentionally sacrificed as a price worth paying for some greater good.

In short, the self-defense precedent, as well as our most familiar institutions of capital punishment and war, show that we permit preventive killing in Newgarth. Therefore, I hold the present defendant to be not guilty of murder, on the ground that the killing he and his comrades intentionally performed was properly preventive. Without it, all six of them would have died. This is equivalent to saying that this killing was necessary, or that it was a bargain, or that a rational person in the same circumstances would have acted as these spelunkers acted. It can easily be distinguished from the case of the killed workmen, which was not a bargain, by the absence of necessity in the latter. At least no one has produced evidence that if the ten workmen had not died, then all sixteen (workmen plus spelunkers) would have died. Consequently, if the workmen had been intentionally killed, we would hunt down the intentional killers and prosecute them.

II

Justice Burnham made one important argument that Justice Springham did not adequately answer. Even on the supposition that the spelunkers would have died without eating one of their companions, only *cannibalism* was necessary for them to live; *homicide* was not. They could have eaten the body of the first of them to die of natural causes. If waiting for that death would permit them to avoid killing, wouldn't that, rather than killing, be truly necessary?

Let me answer this objection directly. No, they need not and should not have waited for the first of them to die of natural causes. Either the spelunkers were roughly of equal fitness, health, and vigor, or they were not. If they were, then by the time the first of them died of starvation, the others would be on the brink of death themselves and unable to take advantage of that fortuitous death. If they were not roughly equal in vigor, then waiting for the first natural death is equivalent to targeting the weakest of their number for death – the sickest, the skinniest, or the one most injured in the landslide. This is not at all an improvement over a fair lottery.

Imagine what issues were raised during the long discussion of the mathematics of the lottery. There are really no mathematical issues in their lottery that are not fairness issues. Their discussion was inevitably about how to be fair with each other in finding a person to kill and eat, given that no one was volunteering.

Isn't it likely that each of them dreaded the prospect of killing and eating a companion? Isn't it likely, therefore, that they sought every alternative before settling on that one? Isn't it likely, therefore, that they considered waiting for the first natural death? Why would they discard that possibility? I can hear the weakest of their number making this plea: "This is just your way of selecting *me*! You *know* I will be the first to die. This is not *fair*! If we each have an equal right to live and eat, then we must each shoulder an equal risk of being selected to feed the rest." This logic is unanswerable to fair-minded people. Indeed, we must commend the spelunkers for recognizing it.

I can even imagine that Whetmore proposed the lottery in the first place precisely because he saw himself as the weakest member of the party and the one most likely to die first unless they adopted a plan to spread the risk more fairly among them. However, this conjecture is not supported by any evidence and has no bearing on the verdict.

My colleagues like Justice Burnham, who believe that waiting for the first natural death was preferable to the affirmative act of killing, stop short in their analysis. They are right that such a course of action would have made killing unnecessary, but they are wrong to think it would have been better than a lottery. It would target the weakest member of the group without the slightest effort to make the risk of sacrifice equal among them. That would resemble the savage "street murder" much more closely than the current case, which is striking for the restraint and level-headedness shown by the spelunkers in spite of their desperation. Most importantly, it would revert to the rule of the weak by the strong, which exists where law does not exist, and which our ancestors abolished in this territory when they signd the second contract that established our Commonwealth.

The rest of the argument has already been given by Justice Springham. The method of selecting the victim was fair because it was random, not because it was consensual. Because Whetmore was chosen by a fair lottery, he was fairly chosen.

III

Now that we have shown that a fair lottery makes consent unnecessary as a method of selecting a victim, we may address one remaining anxiety of those who would use Whetmore's lack of consent to convict the spelunkers.

I have pointed out that killing in self-defense is excused even when the self-defender did not have the consent of the aggressor. Furthermore, we need not think that the aggressor *assumed the risk* of death by his aggression, and consented in that indirect manner to his own death. Killing in self-defense is justified even if we cannot in any way construe the aggressor to have consented; the justification for killing in self-defense cases is self-defense itself, not consent. Moreover, as Justice Springham has correctly pointed out, consent is not a defense to murder in any.

But some of my colleagues still wish to give weight to the fact that Whetmore revoked his consent to join the lottery. If we agree with Springham that Whetmore's consent to join the lottery would not mitigate the crime of the defendant, if it is a crime at all, then we must also accept the converse proposition, that his revocation of consent did not aggravate the crime of the defendant, if it is a crime at all.

Putting that issue to one side, now, we are ready to see the one sense in which

Whetmore's consent or lack of it might be germane to this case. If he was unwilling to join the lottery, for whatever reason, then, the argument goes, he should not have been conscripted into it. He might have been allowed to sit out the lottery in a corner, equally free from the risk of being killed and the obligation to kill, on the condition that he not partake of the flesh of the chosen victim. Why not proceed without him and let him take his chances with hunger if that is what he wanted?

Here is a direct answer to that question. If Whetmore is dropped from the lottery – if his revocation of consent is respected – then each of those remaining would notice, or ought to notice, that his own chance of being selected for death rises from one-sixth to one-fifth. This observation would only tend to increase the chances that another member would withdraw from the pact. If a second spelunker did withdraw, then the chance of losing the lottery would rise again, to one-fourth, making further desertions even more likely. At the limit, the lottery plan would be discarded and there would be nothing left but to wait for starvation or rescue.

What does this prove? It proves that Whetmore's revocation of consent was *not* a good reason to drop him from the lottery. Dropping him would increase the pressure on others to drop out, and therefore increase the chance of destroying the entire lottery plan. But that is to increase the chance of targeting their weakest member for death rather than spreading the risk equally among themselves. In short, if justice required spreading that risk equally, then it required them to ignore Whetmore's revocation of consent. Or to put this in different terms, the spelunkers were justified in conscripting Whetmore into the lottery, even after his revocation of consent, because they were justified in preferring a lottery to a death-watch for their weakest companion.

IV

My colleagues enjoy repeating the obvious and uncontested fact that all six men in the cave were innocent or, in the alternative, that they enjoyed an equal right to live. They say this in order to distinguish the present killing from a killing in self-defense. But, as I have argued, even though this is not a case of self-defense, it is instructive to meditate on self-defense in order to understand the issues of this case. In true self-defense we have one aggressor and one innocent person in a struggle for life; the aggressor's aggression means that one must die; we decide on policy grounds that the death of the aggressor is either a good or the lesser of two evils. In short, the two do *not* enjoy an equal right to live. Deciding who has the greater right to live is the hard part, doctrinally, so wedded are we to the view that all lives are equal in the eyes of the law. Now when we shift to the present facts where all parties are admittedly equal in worth and rights, we see that the doctrinal difficulty of self-defense does not arise. If two of these spelunkers were locked in a struggle for life, when neither could be called the aggressor, then we would have no basis to prefer one to the other. But that is not the hard case we face. Instead we face the much easier case in which one innocent life is sacrificed to save five. The number five is not magical; it could be any number greater than one. Because each life is equal, we have no trouble deciding where public policy places its preference. The law has no basis to prefer one innocent person to another, but it has excellent reasons to prefer five innocent persons to one when circumstances make that choice necessary. This is not profound; all we need is the ability to count.

V

I have argued that this killing was necessary, and to that extent I endorse the analysis of Justice Springham. However, I cannot accept Springham's characterization of the doctrine of necessity. He argues that necessity negates *mens rea* or criminal intent. But this is to make necessity an excuse when it is properly a justification. An excuse exculpates by showing that the defendant is blameless, or lacks criminal intent, even if the defendant's act is harmful and just the one prohibited by the legislature. A justification exculpates by showing that the defendant's act was either good or the lesser evil, even if the defendant's decision to perform that act was free and intentional.

If negating *mens rea* were the proper function of the necessity defense, then the spelunkers would win their defense if they had a good faith belief in the necessity of their homicidal expedient; they would not need to prove that their belief was reasonable in the circumstances. For good faith belief is enough to prove that one lacks criminal intent or willfulness. And clearly, these men did have such a good faith belief. But as Burnham and Springham both show, mere good faith belief in necessity cannot suffice to acquit a person of murder; else we are at the mercy of crackpots whose good faith beliefs exceed the limits of reasonableness. It follows that necessity is not an excuse that negates criminal intent.

Necessity is a justification, not an excuse. If we are dealing with a justification, then we ask whether the act was the lesser evil. Was this killing the lesser evil faced by the spelunkers? To frame the question is to answer it. We know that this killing was the lesser evil just as firmly as we know that one death is less than six.

To see necessity as a justification, not an excuse, is to admit that the spelunkers had, or may as well have had, the criminal intent of murderers. This fact immediately frees us from the hair-splitting we have seen on this bench. We may admit at least for the sake of argument that this killing was willful. It is justified not because willfulness was absent, but because public policy supports any person in choosing the lesser evil over the greater evil, even if they make that choice with intent, deliberation, or willfulness. Necessity is a general defense that need not be mentioned in a specific criminal statute to have validity and effect.

So though the murder statute makes willfulness the test of culpability, a sound necessity defense can acquit even those defendants who acted willfully.

Justices Truepenny and Burnham note that executive clemency is our chosen method for mitigating the rigors of the law. It is one method, to be sure. But the defense of necessity is another and superior method. It is superior to clemency for three reasons. First, the necessity defense is within the reach of judges and juries, not just the executive. So if we find it applicable, we may apply it without bureaucratic or demeaning importunities to another branch of government, sent through the front door or back. Second, the necessity defense is just, not merely merciful. Citizens who believe that the spelunkers should not be punished, even if they violated the letter of our law, are not demanding mercy; they are demanding justice. Third, the necessity defense is law; the people and parties rightfully expect us to follow it; a defendant might deserve to be acquitted under its terms; it has public and justiciable criteria; it is argued in open court and adjudicated on the merits. Clemency is none of these things; it is discretionary and may be granted or withheld capriciously; its criteria are subjective to the executive; it is a form of leniency that is always a gift beyond desert; it cannot be deserved. If the executive pardons the defendant or commutes his sentence, then she will have spared one living defendant from foreseeable injustice, which is so far to the good; but we will not have eliminated the injustice from the rules of law that convicted him in the first place. To acquit him because his act was necessary, or because he acted with legal justification, is truly to mitigate the rigors of the law, and to do so with articulation and accountability; to pardon him because the law is too harsh is no more than gratuitous mercy.

For all the reasons preceding, I vote to overturn the conviction of the trial court, and to acquit the defendant.

OPINION OF JUSTICE HELLEN

I

When a rapist puts a knife blade to a woman's throat and says, *submit or die*, he is giving her a choice. So when she submits, she chooses. Can he therefore claim that she consented? I doubt that anyone thinks so abstractly about consent and choice. Certainly our law does not. If choosing submission over death is a choice that implies consent, then rape would not exist; any woman who survived forced sex would have consented. If our law took this view, then women would be *unrapable* – the term used in centuries past when a wife or prostitute's consent was irrebuttably presumed.

But according to our law, a woman who chooses submission over death or injury does not consent; or, as courts often put it, any consent forced by threat of death or injury is invalid. I remind us of this familiar fact because my colleagues seem to have forgotten it; at least they refuse to draw the lesson from it for the issues of necessity, choice, intent, and willfulness in the present case, illustrating how they systematically avert their eyes from the archetypal crime of violence against women.

A woman who submits to sexual intercourse, when the alternative is death or injury, is being forced, coerced, compelled: she faces "necessity." Necessity explains why her decision to submit does not amount to consent; for the same reasons, it also explains why the spelunkers' decision to kill is not willful. She may act on this necessity in a panic and confusion or with a clear head and full intent; either way, she does not consent. She does not lose her complaint just because she may *knowingly* and *deliberately* prefer life to death. The necessity defense, similarly, belongs just as much to the clear-headed as to the confused, to the intentional as much as to the impulsive.

Rape proves that we can intend an act (submission to a rapist) against our will (without willfulness). This is obvious in the case of rape; but once noticed, we begin to see the same distinction everywhere. For example, the robber who demands, *your money or your life*, offers the victims a choice. Those who choose to give their money rather than die are not thereby making gifts. If they were, there would be no robbery; people would be *unrobbable*.

Similarly, killing in self-defense is not always instinctual or impulsive, immediate and unreflective. Often it has this character because the would-be killer gives the would-be victim no time to reflect. But our courts have often acquitted defendants who did have time to reflect, and who decided in that time intentionally, knowingly, and voluntarily to save their own lives by killing their attackers. These killings are still excused as self-defense. Hence even a killing can be intentional but not willful.

Extortion proves the point from yet another angle. Aristotle gives the example of a tyrant who coerces a good man into performing a wicked deed by threatening to kill his father if he does not comply. Hearing the quandary stated is all we need to feel the man's pain and anger. But in what do this pain and anger consist, or the pain and anger of a rape victim? They consist largely in the lucidity one retains; they consist in the fact that one has been forced to *intend* an act that is *against one's will*.

It is just so with the five spelunkers. They killed with knowledge and deliberation, with intent. But that does not at all mean that they killed willfully. On the contrary, they clearly killed without willfulness; they would rather have taken any other course if only it would have helped them to survive. When they decided that survival required them to kill, they were clear-headed about the necessity of it and spent good time discussing the mathematical issues of a fair lottery. There is no need to punish these men for keeping their heads in a difficult situation, and acting with deliberation and knowledge, any more than a clear-headed woman must be unrapable or a clear-headed traveler unrobbable. Clear-headed deliberation indicates intent, not willfulness. Let us acknowledge that the preference for life over death may be lucid rather than instinctual, and that the actions we undertake to evade death may be intentional rather than impulsive. And let us acknowledge that even a lucid intention to act may be channeled by the limited array of our options, may be forced by the prospect of death, and may be against one's will. To deny this is to forget the obvious lessons of rape, robbery, and extortion, crimes whose essence is to extract a choice from an unwilling victim, a choice that cannot, therefore, be considered willful.

II

My colleagues who are so sure that this isn't a case of self-defense have not been paying attention to the recent evolution of self-defense law, perhaps because women are at center stage in that evolution. The so-called "battered woman's defense" is a recent variation on the theme of self-defense. This variation waives the ancient requirement that the self-defender face "imminent" death or serious bodily injury. A pre-emptive killing may now, in principle, count as self-defense if the defendant can show a history of physical abuse in the aggressor that renders future life-threatening abuse highly probable.

This variation is so recent, in fact, that the four defendants in *Spelunkers I* could not have appealed to it. But that is no reason to close our eyes to its implications for the present defendant or, indeed, for the original four.

I am not arguing that the spelunkers killed in pre-emptive self-defense or that their act falls under the battered woman's defense. I do claim that, if we waive the imminence requirement for battered women, then we may do so for the spelunkers and thereby stop quibbling about whether they waited until the *very last moment* before facing the necessity to kill – as if they, or we, would know what the very last moment was. I also claim that the creative and progressive change of law is not restricted to ancient times, when the exception for self-defense was carved out of our murder statute. Springham was right that, if we accept self-defense as a justification for killing, then we should also accept the analogous defense of self-preservation. This may be an innovation in what we explicitly accept, but it follows directly from what we have already accepted. In short, if the battered woman's defense is a justification for killing, then we are only a small and negligible step away from recognizing a general defense that protects threatened life even when the threat is not immediate.

Here is another invitation to exercise our imagination along similar lines. Imagine that Whetmore had a private stash of food in his backpack but refused to share it. We could stand on abstract property rights, and let him keep it to himself even if that meant that the others would starve. Or we could hold, as we do in every area of law where it comes up, that one may not take a human life in order to protect mere property. On this line of thinking, the law might well require Whetmore to share his provisions. A selfish assertion of his property rights, unless overridden by force or persuasion, would kill his companions. If they had to kill him to share in his stash, I can imagine a responsible court interpreting that act as self-defense.* Obviously we need not decide that case today. The lesson is not that hoarding can be homicide, but that law changes and self-defense law changes. The fact that historical models of self-defense are unavailable to the spelunkers is a fact of only historical interest.

Several colleagues argue that this is not a case of self-defense because Whetmore was not an aggressor. But no one has ever denied Whetmore's innocence. Why are my colleagues fighting without an antagonist? Self-defense is a species of necessity; and while the innocence of the victim is usually material in self-defense cases, it is never material in necessity cases. If we shift the label from "self-defense" to "necessity," then Whetmore's innocence becomes irrelevant. Springham uses the good example of the tenant breaking the landlord's windows to escape from a fire. This destruction of private property is justified by necessity. The landlord may be entirely innocent. It is the fire, not the landlord, that makes the tenant's act necessary. Similarly, Whetmore was blameless; it was extreme

---

* Similar life v. property issues were earlier raised by Professor Wun, a member of the Special Commission established by the executive after *Spelunkers I* to decide whether to recommend clemency. D'Amato, *op. cit.* at p. 472.

hunger, not any fault of Whetmore's, that made killing a human being necessary. Whetmore was the victim because he had the bad luck to lose the dice throw, not because of any fault of his own. We cannot blame the spelunkers for picking one of their number at random to kill, once we acknowledge the necessity to kill someone, any more than we can blame the tenant in the burning building for breaking this window, rather than that one, in order to escape.

Finally, it has long been the law in our Commonwealth that the right of self-defense includes the right to kill an innocent person in some circumstances. If A attacks B with fatal force, and B defends with fatal force, accidentally shooting bystander C instead of aggressor A, then B is still entitled to acquittal on the ground of self-defense. Again, I am not arguing that the spelunkers killed Whetmore accidentally, while aiming at the true aggressor responsible for their predicament. Let us admit that Whetmore was innocent, but stop citing his innocence as if it ruled out an argument from self-defense or necessity.

In short, the defendant killed from necessity and must be acquitted of the charge of murder. Whether we call the necessity under which he acted "self-defense" is not legally significant. Self-defense is one kind of necessity; there are other kinds, without names, that are arbitrarily close to self-defense in their moral and political rationale. It also happens that the law of self-defense has expanded and mutated in recent years under the influence of woman-responsive jurisprudence. To assert that the defendant's homicide was justified by self-defense fits recent developments, or legitimately extends them, and should not be denied merely because such an outcome would have been novel when most of my "brothers" were in law school.

III

Does the case of *Commonwealth v. Valjean* negate the spelunkers' necessity defense? If Valjean could not argue necessity to justify the theft of bread, then how can the spelunkers argue necessity to justify homicide? I admire Justice Springham's detailed attempt to distinguish *Valjean* from the present case (at p. 49, above); I cannot imagine anyone doing a better job. However, it is unnecessary to distinguish a case that is no longer valid law. Justice Tatting was right that arguments to acquit the spelunkers on the ground of necessity entail that we overturn *Valjean* (see p.18, above). So let us take the direct and effective course of overturning *Valjean* once and for all. *Valjean* reflects the class biases of a Court, indeed, an entire system of criminal justice, for which desperate poverty and chronic homelessness are abstract fictions. True, some homeless people can beg, and others can obtain food from charities, but for a government to demand these expedients from the desperate poor when its police shoo beggars out of sight and its legislature bars the public support of religious charities is cynical and morally evasive. Moreover, it assumes that private charities will always suffice to keep the poor from desperate acts such as Valjean's. This is an empirical question that is not settled by the serene confidence of the Supreme Court. Sometimes this assumption is true, and, when it is true, we have private generosity to thank, not the Commonwealth. But sometimes it is false, and, when it is false, justice requires the Commonwealth to take notice. *Valjean* was wrongly decided. Starvation is a paramount form of necessity; when it cannot be alleviated within the law, then alleviating it outside the law does not carry the culpable criminal intent which alone we must punish. Instead, like other cases of *bona fide* necessity, it carries the peremptory will to live that precedes all law.

IV

The necessity defense is one way that we acknowledge and respond to the fallibility of legislators. By permitting a necessity defense at all, we are admitting that to follow the letter of the law can occasionally work an injury or injustice. The necessity defense is designed for defendants who violate the law in order to avoid just such injuries or injustices. They took a legal risk to do what we can agree is right; they ought to be spared punishment. It is a mistake, therefore, to make the necessity defense into another technical doctrine with a "letter of the law" all its own, as both Burnham and Springham do from their respective sides. Because judges are fallible too, if we codify the necessity defense in black-letter law, then to follow the letter of *that* law might also, in unforeseen circumstances, work an injury or injustice.

The proper test of necessity, then, is not to look for a precisely formulated rule from our cases, or to formulate our own, but to assess with courage and candor the injustice the defendant tried to avoid by his unlawful act. We ought to take the measure of that injustice using the common sense and norms of the general community, since it is the general community's policy to avoid injustice that we are trying to enforce here. The community governs through the web of legal rules, and only a near-sighted focus on the rules can obscure that fact. By this test, the defendant is clearly not guilty, even if his act was willful. The evil he sought to avoid was his own death, which our community norms – and our case law too – declare to be more than sufficient to justify the use of fatal force.

V

If all my arguments above are flawed, and the defendant is guilty of a technical violation of our murder statute, then what good would be achieved by punishing him? Surely retribution is inappropriate for a defendant without evil will; and even law-and-order retributivists, like Burnham, are not willing to say that any of the spelunkers had evil will. Nor must society protect itself from citizens like these spelunkers. If they have shown themselves willing to kill, it is only after several weeks trapped under the earth with no food; they are not a threat to society.

Finally, I would like to point out the absurdity of supposing that a guilty verdict in this case would deter others similarly situated. The impossibility of deterring acts of this kind is evident in our very recognition that this act was forced by necessity or occurred without willfulness. Even the most virtuous spelunker will have to eat, and eventually will be pushed by starvation to the point of necessity at which he will kill in spite of the considerations that deter less desperate people. When a person is pushed to that point, deterrence is impossible, killing is necessary, and killing is excusable under the law; these are all ways of saying the same thing.

The execution of the four defendants from *Spelunkers I* was controversial and widely discussed. Let us assume that the verdict in that case, and the punishment, are universally known among Newgarthian spelunkers, as major events of speluncean interest. Any Newgarthian spelunkers who might be inside a cave on this very day, will know, then, that killing a companion for food is regarded as murder, even when the extremity of starvation is conceded.

Can we say that the previous verdicts and executions will exert any deterrent effect on present and future Newgarthian spelunkers who are genuinely pushed to the extremity of starvation and necessity? Clearly not. What it *means* to be pushed to the extremity of necessity is that one would then kill another to save oneself.

Even if *Spelunkers I* had an insignificant deterrent effect, perhaps it had a slight effect in the direction of deterrence. Would we amplify its deterrent effect if we upheld the jury's conviction of the present defendant? Again, clearly not. We would merely clarify, or perhaps only reiterate, that trapped and starving spelunkers face death: for they will die either by starvation or by execution. But if these are one's only options, then it becomes rational, even necessary, to kill to avoid starvation and take one's chances at beating execution, say, with a novel defense. The disagreements on this Court, if not the exigencies of starvation, give hope to this strategy.

Yet if punishing the defendant would not serve the ends of retribution, self-protection, or deterrence, then it would not serve the purposes of punishment. And to punish when the ends of punishment are not served is to make a fetish of rule-following and to forget the reason for the rules. My colleagues describe the horror of this case of desperation, homicide, and cannibalism, but in the end it has still not sunk in; they act much more like little boys playing a game who become so carried away by their dispute about the rules that they forget why they are playing.

VI

I have two questions to ask my colleagues who believe that the defendant is guilty beyond a reasonable doubt.

First, do we know beyond a reasonable doubt that a person at the point of death by starvation possesses the mental capacity to commit willful murder? Did this defendant? His physical deterioration, with the faintness caused by extreme hunger, augmented by natural fear and anxiety, easily surpasses the threshold we require in other cases for an exculpatory diminution of mental capacity.

Against this view one may cite the lengthy discussion of the mathematics of the lottery. But this is far from conclusive evidence. If the mathematical discussion was clear-headed and competent, then it no more suggests willfulness than the lucidity of the woman who sees the knife, draws the inference, and intentionally but unwillingly submits to the rapist. But if the mathematical discussion was not clear-headed or competent, then it suggests that the mental faculties of the spelunkers were clouded by incapacity, hunger, and panic. After all, the mathematics of a fair lottery are relatively simple, especially if dice are present as in this case. We will never have sufficient evidence to assess the mental state of the men in the cave at the time of the killing, but we do have sufficient evidence to create reasonable doubt of willfulness.

We might even conclude from these considerations that a guilty verdict will have the opposite effect of deterrence. The lesson to a starving spelunker who has managed to retain a glimmer of sense is to crouch in a corner of the cave, engage in no mathematical discussions and no lottery, wait until starvation is unendurable, and then leap up screaming and stab a companion 114 times. This would establish a defense of insanity or diminished capacity and eliminate all the confusion caused by the spelunkers' supposed lack of confusion.

Second, are my colleagues too caught up in their quarrel over guilt and innocence to see that the quarrel itself has a decisive implication for the case?

Can a *divided* Supreme Court *fairly* rule that there is no reasonable doubt of someone's guilt? Under the rules, yes. In what law students call "real life," clearly not. In real life, an appellate court divided on the question whether there is reasonable doubt of someone's guilt proves the existence of reasonable doubt. Technically, a divided jury does not acquit, but it does prevent conviction through a mistrial. A divided Supreme Court should be at least as favorable to the defendant. When we divide on the very question whether a doubt is reasonable, then we know that at least one Supreme Court justice believes there is reasonable doubt of guilt. If this does not of itself establish the existence of reasonable doubt, then it should at least prevent conviction through an analogue to mistrial that we may call *misappeal*. The only alternative is to suppose that the doubts of an average Supreme Court justice are less reasonable than those of an average juror. (Of course, if we really believed this, we would not permit appeals.)

How can educated people fall into such a trap? The trap is to mistake law for a system of rules. On this view, law is abstract, not concrete; timeless, not historical; a deposit of rationality, not a continuing struggle of multi-dimensional human beings; a bloodless structure of logic, not the raw and refined material of life itself; an artificial game, not a social reality. On this view, law is like a computer program, and it is entirely regrettable that it must be executed by slow, fallible, interested, and emotional human judges rather than by fast, infallible, disinterested, and unemotional machines. But also on this view, ironically, reasonable doubt cannot be established by the reasoned arguments of Supreme Court justices, only by the votes of jurors, which may well be entirely emotional. Our policy would be a comical self-deception if its consequences were not so often tragic.

Is it too much to hope that the highly educated members of this Court will see what is obvious, if that means looking through the web of rules to the reality beyond? Four Supreme Court justices who think there is reasonable doubt of guilt prove that there is reasonable doubt of guilt, even if they are not a majority. Therefore, we must acquit.

VII

Justice Burnham argues that judges should follow the law, not their own private notions of justice, because in a pluralistic society the people may agree on the laws and disagree on the requirements of justice (see pp. 43ff, above). He has strong words for anyone, or at least any judge, who would appeal to justice beyond law. I have made several appeals to justice as reasons to revise or extend our law; hence I ought to face Burnham's argument and answer it squarely. Actually, Burnham makes a strong argument that I would embrace if we lived in the good, pluralistic society where he imagines us to live. His only mistake is to claim that we really live in his fantasy-world of civil rationality. He admits (at p. 43, above) that his argument only works "as long as we take pains to let all views be heard in the law-making process." His argument fails to the extent that Newgarthian society has failed to live up to this participatory ideal; and this failure is distressingly large and long-standing.

The weakness of Burnham's argument may come clear with an analogy. A commonplace of our political rhetoric holds that civil disobedience is not justified in a democracy, for protesters with a grievance may petition the legislature and the public for relief. If their reasons are good ones, and their numbers large, then they will prevail without violating the law; but if their reasons are not good ones, or their numbers small, then they do not deserve to prevail. This argument is attractive because it, or something very much like it, is true of the ideal society in which we hope to live. Good reasons and real numbers ought to matter, but it does not follow that they do matter where we do live. Burnham's argument assumes that the legislature properly reflects the entire population, but this assumption founders on what we know of the disproportionate influence of wealth and privilege on real elections and real legislation. We can only tell activists who would perform civil disobedience to leave the streets, go home, and write letters to their legislators, if the system is already just. Similarly, Burnham can dismiss appeals to justice beyond law with his characteristic air of righteousness only if the law is already just. But if the law is shaped by interest, wealth, and power, not by pluralistic voices in proportion to their numbers and reasonableness, then Burnham's argument functions as a rationale for ignoring these pleas for change; hence it functions as a rationale for entrenching injustice. If law institutionalizes privilege, then it cannot "let all views be heard in the lawmaking process." We do not live in Burnham's pluralistic society, where groups with different views and interests have reached a "meta-level agreement" on the rightness of law; we live in a pluralistic society where some views and interests simply dominate over others. As long as that is the case, appeals to justice beyond law are our only hope of bringing justice and law into alignment.

I vote to overturn the conviction and acquit the defendant.

OPINION OF JUSTICE
TRUMPET

I

My colleagues seem to agree that the chief question in this case is the defense of necessity. Hence, they pile up argument after argument on the question whether the spelunkers killed from necessity. But they have entirely misunderstood the case. Necessity cannot justify or excuse the killing of a human being, as I will show shortly. Hence we need not even reach the question whether the spelunkers killed from necessity; all the labor that Burnham and Springham and the others have spent in this cause is labor lost.

Springham admits what is obvious, that this is not a case of self-defense. But he says it is a case of "self-preservation" instead (at p. 46, above), as if the new phrase brought its own illumination. Hellen thinks the case is some yet-unnamed variation of self-defense (at pp. 65f, above), as if the association with so ancient a justification as self-defense lent validity to her claim without more ado. But this case is not about necessity or self-preservation or self-defense. It is about equality. Or if it is about some right of self-preservation, then it is about the unequal recognition of that right inside the cave. The surviving spelunkers placed a higher value on their own lives than they placed on the life of Roger Whetmore. This Court cannot pretend that the state of Newgarth and its laws support this violent and self-serving inequality.

Each life is supremely and infinitely valuable in the eyes of the law. This fact makes them of equal value. None takes priority over others. Any sacrifice must be voluntary or else violate the equality and sanctity of life recognized by our laws. When there is no volunteer, there is no right to kill non-volunteers. Each person has a duty to die before killing another in violation of this highest moral and legal obligation.

Springham and Tally attempt to show that the lottery put the equal rights of the spelunkers on an equal footing (at pp. 52 and 59ff, above). While this is true as far as it goes, it overlooks the fact that the purpose of the lottery was to kill the loser for the benefit of the winners. The purpose was to enforce the ultimate inequality. The unequal outcome cannot be defended on the ground that each spelunker had an equal chance of suffering it, for the simple reason that equality cannot be twisted to justify inequality.

The relevant principle here is that first articulated by Socrates (in the *Gorgias*), that it is better to suffer injustice than to do injustice. Or it is that later articulated by Jesus (in *Luke*), that if one strikes you on the cheek, you should offer the other one. These are the "religious fanatics" (see p. 58, above) who dissent from Tally's repulsive view that killing can be a bargain.

On these grounds, we may cut through the confusion surrounding the ancient precedent on self-defense. My colleagues wonder why our early judges recognized self-defense as an exception to the murder statute when our early legislators refused to do so. My colleagues speculate that killing in self-defense is excused because it is not willful, because it is deeply ingrained in our nature, because punishing self-defenders will not deter, because self-defense is preventive killing, or because self-defense is not covered by the purpose of our murder statute. But all this is speculation.

Killing in self-defense violates the principle to suffer injustice before committing it. This is a principle of natural law. Repeated violations do not amend it. For colleagues who have lost their way, and cannot discern an eternal law when it conflicts with human interest, the same conclusion follows from human law. Killing in self-defense violates the plain and literal meaning of our murder statute, which would punish all willful killings. A nation devoted to "the principle of the supremacy of the legislature" (Justice Keen at p. 21, above) cannot tolerate judicial qualifications to unqualified legislative language.

Self-defense was excluded by the murder statute for the best of reasons: the framers did not want self-defense to excuse killing. They believed that one should turn the other cheek. Let me be explicit: the ancient precedent exempting self-defense from the murder statute was wrongly decided and should be overturned. I know that I lack the votes to overturn it, however, and I do not expect to have the votes in my lifetime. Moreover, respect for precedent may require that I acquiesce in the judicial invention, at least after this long a time. But I must press the principle that repudiates self-defense because it is still part of our law and it bears directly on the case of these unfortunate spelunkers.

Mr Staymore was prevented by physical force from obeying a parking ordinance; compliance was impossible. The spelunkers were not *prevented* from obeying the law at all; they were *tempted* to disobey, and they found that they were too weak to resist the temptation. They found disobedience a more attractive option than obedience. Obedience was far from impossible because their crime was far from necessary. Obedience was possible but horrible to contemplate. Have men a right to avoid the horrible? Even if we accept the view that they do, we cannot accept it in defense of killing a man, for that act is at least as horrible as starving to death, the act from which they were fleeing.

Justice Springham accuses Justice Burnham of disliking the necessity defense (at p. 52, above), just as Keen accuses Foster of disliking statutes (at p. 22, above). But because we have a necessity defense and statutes, we are supposed to conclude that Burnham and Foster are simply at odds with the laws they are sworn to uphold. This would be damaging if true. But the fact is that, while we do have statutes, we do not have a necessity defense in Newgarth. More precisely, we have a necessity defense for overparking, as proved by *Staymore*, which has never been questioned. But I ask Justice Springham where in our case law he finds authority for the chilling claim that we have a necessity defense for homicide. (We have no necessity defense for cannibalism because, as Justice Tatting pointed out, at p. 19 above, we have no statute criminalizing cannibalism.) Justice Burnham dislikes the necessity defense because it justifies violating the law and carries an inherent risk of anarchy. Springham's reply admits the risk and offers in exchange to read the defense narrowly, requiring reasonable belief, rather than merely good faith belief, in the necessity (at p. 49, above). Springham's position is essentially that Burnham prefers order to justice, while justice requires a necessity defense regardless of its consequences for order.

But Springham is wrong. Justice never requires us to kill, even when necessary to prevent our own deaths. Justice requires that we should die before we kill. I wish to be spared the wailing of intentional killers who claim that justice required them to kill; the odor offends. I say to the defendant that he should voluntarily have starved to death. This is a hard saying, which I do not make lightly or flippantly. But when the alternative is to kill a human being, it is clearly the course required by justice. More shameful than the spelunkers surviving their accident is Springham's claim that "justice" permits the killing of Roger Whetmore. It would be better to argue that justice should be put to one side than that justice supports their decision to kill.

Springham says the method of selecting the victim was fair because it was random, not because it was consensual (at p. 52, above). This follows, he says, from our rule of law that consent of the victim is not a defense to murder. What Springham does not say is that according to his principles this killing would be equally fair if the victim selected at random had gone to his death kicking and screaming. If consent is irrelevant, and random selection is all we demand for fairness, then I invite my colleagues to imagine with particularity the scene in which a vigorously resisting victim is grabbed, held down, and killed. This is *fair*?

Moreover, while we do not know the method of killing, we do know that Whetmore did not consent. We may presume, therefore, that he did resist, to the limit of his strength. We do not know how strong he was on the day of his death, but his resistance must have put his killers to a some effort to secure him and end his life. Can the spelunkers admit to exerting this effort and energy and still maintain that they were on the very brink of death by starvation and unable to wait even one more day?

Springham says the men killed in "self-preservation" and admits that Whetmore does not meet the test of an aggressor for the purposes of self-defense. But if these ordinary, unlucky mortals can kill a person not specifically threatening them, because they would die without the nourishment of that person's flesh, then why can't a citizen with kidney disease kill the hapless owner of a kidney of matching tissue-type, and take one of the victim's kidneys for transplantation?* Or if there is more than one potential donor of matching tissue-type, why not pick one of them by a fair lottery, kill the loser, and take a kidney? The healthy kidney owner is no more, and no less, innocent than Roger Whetmore, and the citizen with kidney disease is no more, and no less, moved by necessity than these spelunkers. We do not believe that anyone deserves to die of kidney failure, any more than to die in a landslide. When it happens, we mourn for the victims and their families. Yet when there are no voluntary donors, we tell people with kidney disease that they must die rather than create an involuntary donor through murder. We must say the same to these spelunkers.

They are guilty of murder. No examination of the morality of their act can cut against this conclusion, for they are as guilty morally as they are legally. Indeed, the principle of the sanctity of life is a moral principle first and a legal principle second. Attempts to find this killing morally justified, for example through necessity or variations on self-defense, or to separate the law and morality of murder, violate both the morals and the laws of Newgarth.

II

Justice Tally is simply wrong (at p. 58, above) that all his colleagues secretly believe that killing one person to save five is a bargain. I am one who thinks it is barbaric. But because the argument from numbers is on many minds, and functions as a sticking point even for clear thinkers, it deserves an answer. Could we kill one to save a hundred? A million? Is there a point at which the "gain" from killing exceeds the "loss" and we can begin to speak of a "bargain"?

Tally would kill one to save five, and one to save a million. But would he kill four to save five? How about 999,999 to save 1,000,000? I imagine that even his callous intuition would begin to balk at these numbers, although according to his bloodless arithmetic the "bargain" is as obvious in each case.

If all lives are of infinite worth, then one life is as valuable as two. One is as valuable as a million. In fact, one is as valuable as an infinite number. There is never a bargain in preventive killing; there are only survivors with blood on their hands.

I concede that it may often be "necessary" to kill some to save others. By this I mean that, *if* those others are to be saved, *then* some must be killed. I even concede that the spelunkers found themselves in such a situation. But in such situations the killing is only hypothetically necessary: it is necessary only *if* some others are to live. Hypothetical necessities do not suffice here. It is hypothetically necessary for you to be killed if I am to wear your scalp or decorate my desk with your skull. Do I then kill you on the ground of necessity? Obviously not. I

---

* Professor Wun raises a more complex transplantation analogy in D'Amato, *op. cit.* at p. 469.

concede the hypothetical necessity but resign myself to a life in which I do not wear your scalp or decorate my desk with your skull. If some must really be killed to save others, then the others must resign themselves to a much shorter life, rather than a longer one at the expense of their congeners.

Tally's doctrine works only when the units he is counting are of finite worth, for then the value of five always exceeds the value of one. But a life is not such a unit. He will say that the damages we award in wrongful death cases show that we put a finite price on a human life. But if he were right, then we would also allow rich people to buy poor people, and turn anyone into chattel against his will if only the price is paid. It is much easier to explain why we value life infinitely and yet award finite damages for wrongful death than for Tally to explain why his view of human worth is not grounds for the commodification of humanity.

But even if we grant him the view that human lives are of finite worth under the law, his logic does not work in the case of these speluncean explorers. For if we take Tally's logic seriously, then the five lottery winners inside the cave were justified in killing the lottery loser, the sixth spelunker. If at that point an unexpected landslide prolonged the rescue another few weeks, and if the men were given the bad news by radio, then it would only be a matter of time before four of the five survivors would be justified in killing the fifth. If we repeat the landslide and radio communication, then soon three of the four survivors would be justified in killing the fourth, and then two of the three in killing the third. If we repeat one more time, then, finally, one would be justified in killing the other, in the limiting case of preventive killing. By Tally's logic, each of the killings was a bargain; but in the end, one is alive and five are dead and eaten. If we justify killing one to save five, then in the end we justify killing five to save one. Even by Tally's arithmetic, is that a bargain?

III

Justice Hellen is simply wrong that "virtuous" spelunkers will have to eat, even if they have to kill a human being to do so (at p. 69, above). This is the presumptuous statement of a woman who has either never met a virtuous person or failed to take the proper lesson from the encounter. A virtuous person would voluntarily starve to death before killing. This, not killing, is what is necessary in such a dreadful and harrowing situation. Fasting unto death is not easy to undertake, but is its moral necessity really that hard to grasp? The discipline to refrain from murder even at the cost of one's own life is part of what we *mean* by virtue.

IV

Finally, I have not failed to notice that there is a contradiction between the principle of the sanctity of life, which underlies our murder statute, and the mandatory death penalty contained in that statute. The statute is in conflict with itself. This is a very firm ground for nullifying the part of the statute supported by the weaker principle. By "firm" I mean as compared to other grounds often cited by judges for nullifying statutes, such as abstract justice or common sense. The mandatory death penalty may be supported by such principles as self-protection, deterrence (*Parry*), or retribution (*Scape*); but none of these principles has the weight, or the deep roots in our jurisprudence, of the principle of the sanctity of life. Moreover, each of the principles that supports the death penalty may be served to some degree by life imprisonment; hence, the purpose of the statute cannot require the death penalty, regardless of our theory of the purpose of the statute. This shows that the principles supporting the death penalty are less essential to the foundations of Newgarthian law than the principle of the sanctity of life. Hence I would nullify the provision of the murder statute prescribing a mandatory death penalty.

It is too late to save the first four spelunkers from execution, but not too late to recognize the true principle and treat the present defendant, murderer though he be, as a creature of infinite worth, and thereby demonstrate that we do not share his moral principles.

I vote to uphold the conviction, but to remand the case to the Court of General Instances for re-sentencing.

OPINION OF JUSTICE GOAD

I

When the first woman was appointed a Justice of the Supreme Court of Newgarth, nearly one hundred years ago now, most men and very likely a large number of women imagined that she would "speak for women." Indeed, it is not too cynical to suppose that that is precisely why she was appointed. It wasn't until the sixth woman was appointed that Newgarth had two women justices simultaneously. It was only then that most men, and very likely some women, learned that not all women think alike. This was a beneficial turn of events, if it meant that women were becoming a complex reality rather than an empty abstraction. But at the same time it was a calamity, for if not all women think alike, then who would speak for women?

My brothers are tired of being reminded that Justice Hellen and I do not necessarily think alike, any more than (say) Justices Keen and Foster think alike. Justice Hellen herself is probably tired of this fact too, for her written opinions suggest that she is trying to speak for women and assumes that all women think, or ought to think, alike. But I will be tiresome and remind us all of our differences one more time.

There are several reasons why the defendant is guilty of murder. One is that the spelunkers must take some responsibility for the excruciating dilemma in which they found themselves. Another is that Roger Whetmore had a right to defend himself, which is incompatible with the defense theory of necessity. Another, to be succinct, is that *no means no.*

To take the third of these first: Justice Hellen analogizes the surviving spelunkers (at p. 64, above) to rape victims because they were forced to commit an act intentionally but against their will. (Is every case really about rape?) However, even on her terms, she has the situation perfectly reversed. The surviving spelunkers are much more like rapists than rape victims, for they reduced Roger Whetmore to an object (not a sexual object, but a nutritional object), violently subordinated him to their will, and made him serve their interests. His consent or dissent was disregarded, ignored, overridden, written out of the equation. When brutality of this description takes the form of sexual intercourse, it is rape; when it takes the form of intentional killing, it is murder.

Whetmore proposed the lottery and at first undoubtedly consented to its terms. But before the dice were thrown, he just as unmistakably revoked his consent. Did this stop the spelunkers? How many times have we heard that a woman who goes to a man's apartment, or even to dinner with him, has already by her conduct consented to sexual relations? Not all the behaviors that men believe manifest consent do manifest consent. And even a *bona fide* consent is revocable. If this were not so, women would be raised apart from men, wear long black robes and veils, and avert their eyes from every man's gaze. But life is very different because, in fact and in law, *no means no.*

So we start from the principle that consents are revocable. Roger Whetmore revoked his consent to join the lottery. When the spelunkers threw the dice for him, he did not think the dice were loaded or the throw rigged, and he said so, but this was assent to the fairness of the throw, not consent to rejoin the compact. This had no effect on his companions, who killed him as if he had consented.

Some news commentators speculate that Whetmore proposed the lottery intending from the start to withdraw from it at the last moment and then to find a clever way (perhaps by pathetic whimpering) to join the meal that the others purchased through murder.* Of course there is no evidence for this contention. But in any case, it is easily answered by the analysis I have offered above. Even if the speculation were entirely true, it remains a fact that Whetmore did revoke his consent. A woman who willingly shares a dinner with a man is entitled to say *no* after dessert and have it respected. (Does this really require repetition?) The alternative is to say that a woman whose revocation of consent frustrates a man deserves to be raped.

Why did the spelunkers spend so much time discussing the mathematics of the lottery if it was not to obtain the consent of every member of their party? Even if consent is not a defense to murder, as Springham correctly observes, consent was clearly important to the spelunkers. But if so, what excuse do they have for overriding Whetmore's dissent? Whetmore's lack of consent is relevant to this case, not because consent is a defense to murder, but because the spelunkers cannot claim necessity unless they come to court with clean hands. Our sympathy for them depends critically on the cleanliness of their hands, and the justice of acquitting them depends in large part on that sympathy.

I will return to the consent issues in a moment. But first I must point out that when Justice Hellen analogizes the spelunkers to rape victims (at p. 64, above), she is implicitly analogizing Roger Whetmore to a rapist. But this is past absur-

---

* Professor Thri even contends that Whetmore would have a legally compelling argument to take part in the eating, even if he did not take part in the killing. D'Amato, *op. cit.* at p. 484. To deny Whetmore any nutrition at that point could well be construed as murder.

dity. Whetmore did nothing to threaten, harm, or endanger the other spelunkers that each of them did not likewise do to the rest. Each man was alive, hence needy; each man had a body that might serve as food. But in this they were equals; Whetmore was not specifically threatening. This is the same reason why we cannot classify the killing as self-defense. Whetmore was not an aggressor. He is not guilty of anything. If anyone must die, there is no reason why it should be Whetmore and not one of the others. He can only play the role of a rapist, or of an aggressor for a theory of self-defense, even for the novel new women-responsive variations on self-defense, if he threatens the others in a way in which they do not threaten each other.

Let me remind the Court of an appalling chapter in the history of our jurisprudence. Before the state can convict a person of a crime, it must prove a so-called "mental element" or "criminal intent," sometimes simply called *mens rea*. If the defendant lacks *mens rea*, then no crime was committed; if the state fails to prove *mens rea*, then it loses. Once upon a time our predecessors on this Court held that *mens rea* in the crime of rape is for a man to know at the time of sexual intercourse that the woman is not consenting. Hence, if he sincerely believed that the woman did consent, then he lacked *mens rea* and was no rapist. He needed only good faith belief, or sincerity, because this was a question about his state of mind. His belief did not have to be true, or reasonable in the circumstances, or based on a shred of evidence; it only had to be psychologically actual. A man might have a sincere but unreasonable belief in a woman's consent because she gave ambiguous signs or because he was drunk or stupid. He might also be talented in believing what he wants to believe. But as long as he is excused by his state of mind, regardless of the state of mind of his victim, then even women who give unambiguous signs of refusal are at the mercy of such men. All this followed inevitably from received wisdom about the *mens rea* requirement for every crime. This doctrine had the effect of converting a woman's consent into a man's belief about a woman's consent. This result was too transparently oppressive to remain law for long, although we often forget that it took twenty-four years to correct the situation with definitive legislation.

Because Newgarth was founded upon an explicit social contract by the survivors of the ancient holocaust in the first period following the Great Spiral (Foster at p. 12, above), many writers have drawn an analogy between our experiment with rape law and our notion of a social contract. We have on record the express consent of the founding generation to the social contract. But for all their descendants down to the present day we have, at best, only tacit consent. Nowadays our consent is inferred from our conduct, for example, in accepting government benefits and services. For what purpose is our consent inferred? Chiefly, in order to hold us bound to the laws. We still believe that our obligation to obey the laws is grounded, not on a mysterious moral duty, and certainly not on some divine right of our sovereign body, but on our consent to obey them, tacit though it may be. Who infers our consent? The state does, when it must hold us accountable for violating its laws. This is like the appalling rule of "good faith rape," for it has the effect of converting our consent to be governed into the government's belief about our consent. Is this too an oppression to be corrected? Or is it a misreading of the way consent is manifested and ascertained in Newgarth today?

Many writers have answered this grave charge against our form of government, arguing for example that the state plays no essential role in establishing our tacit consent to be governed, since the job could as well be performed by any independent or non-governmental entity, such as a Martian observer, Newgarthian jury, or non-partisan academic sociologist. I need not pass on the effectiveness of these rebuttals to point out that most Newgarthians see that they have an interest in their success. For if the charge is not answered, then our form of government is illegitimate for resting on a spurious form of consent, or a conclusory fiction that constructs consent out of what may as well be dissent.

All this is a roundabout way of pointing out that we have long since repudiated the "good faith rape" rule and try at every opportunity to rebut the charge that our form of government is similarly perverse. But if we really think we have learned our lesson, then we must live up to the lesson we think we have learned. If a woman's consent is not just a man's belief, then we must look for it in the woman. In short, *no means no*. If consent was the basis of the lottery, then Roger Whetmore's consent cannot be inferred or constructed by his killers; it must be looked for in Roger Whetmore. But it is not there to be found, for he revoked his consent and never consented again, as all parties agree.

II

Springham, Tally, and Hellen would argue, I am sure, that killing Whetmore without his consent would not matter, or would be excusable, if the spelunkers acted under necessity. I would like to put the question in a slightly different way: not whether the spelunkers acted under necessity, but what difference it would make if they did. If a man "must" rape a woman in order to be admitted into a gang, we do not let this "necessity" acquit him of the rape. But what if his refusal to commit the rape would cause the gang to kill him, and he knows this? Our lower courts have heard such cases. That new refinement tightens the analogy to the present case. Surely, we do what we must do to avoid death, and this fact lessens or eliminates our *mens rea* for injuries we cause along the way. But in that case, why do we lack sympathy for the would-be gang member caught in this dilemma? Wouldn't we ask how he found himself in the predicament in which he must either rape or die? Does he bear any responsibility for walking up to that choice-point, and hence, for the rape he performs "in order to" escape death? A similar series of questions leads us to deny a necessity defense to the fleeing criminal who finds himself under police fire and grabs an innocent bystander as a hostage or shield. Yes, the criminal's life is threatened, and yes, this recourse will protect him, but no, his responsibility for his quandary bars him from saving his life at the expense of another.

In the present pair of cases, the defendant spelunkers bear a large responsibility. They did not cause the avalanche; nor did they seek out the risk of avalanche for sport. But they voluntarily walked into a hostile natural environment where their range of choices in case of disaster was foreseeably narrow. Why did they do it? Not to avoid death, not to put food on the table, but for enjoyment. We must conclude, then, that their own voluntary acts are largely to blame for the fact that they found themselves in a situation where killing was "necessary" to avoid their own deaths. This fact drains the necessity of their desperate act of its exculpatory power. Moreover, when the final hour came, they chose to save themselves by taking the life of one who was the moral equivalent of an innocent bystander and making him their body shield against hunger.

Why am I not very sympathetic to the spelunkers? First, because they acted as if consent mattered and then they ignored their victim's dissent. Second, because the necessity under which they acted was a product of their voluntary acts. Here I focus on the second of these reasons. I would be much more sympathetic to a group of grocers, dry cleaners, and typists who found themselves trapped in a collapsed building by an earthquake or terrorist bomb. If they eventually killed a member of their group after the same radio communications, the same degree of starvation, the same lottery, and even the same revocation of consent by the lottery loser, then their necessity defense would be much stronger than the one offered by these spelunkers. There might still be good reason to deny it to them, but they would not forfeit it because of their own responsibility for courting or creating the necessity that oppressed them.

Why do we acquit defendants who were involuntarily intoxicated at the time of their criminal acts, but not those who were voluntarily intoxicated? Our theory of criminal intent or *mens rea* seems to require that we acquit them both; they lack the requisite state of mind in exactly the same way and may as well lack it to exactly the same degree. The short answer is that we are much less sympathetic to those who cause harm while voluntarily drunk than to those who cause harm while involuntarily drunk. The reason is clearly that voluntary drunks bear some responsibility both for their intoxicated state and for any harm they cause while in that state. We can say that we are unsympathetic to voluntary drunks because they bear this responsibility for their own loss of mental capacity. Or we can say that bearing this responsibility makes a legal difference because it causes us to lose sympathy for them. It doesn't matter to me whether we justify the legal doctrine through the emotion or through the same facts that justify the emotion, and I have never read an opinion in which it did matter.

The scenario of the gang-member is a true story and true more than once in our recent urban history. It is relevant because it teaches us the limits of the necessity defense. No one pleads necessity to the charge of rape; or if they do, we will not accept their defense. While there is never a true necessity to rape, there can be, as the law of self-defense shows, a true necessity to kill. We learn from the rape analogy when a necessity defense must be rejected on the grounds of the defendant's willing complicity in the causal origin of his dilemma. But the rape analogy is unnecessary to make this point. We learn the same lesson from the now-venerable distinction between the culpability of voluntary drunks and the lack of culpability in involuntary drunks. This lesson clearly works against the spelunkers.

III

I would now like to argue directly against the notion that this killing, or any killing not done in self-defense, can be justified by necessity. Tally rightly corrects Springham on the elementary distinction between an excuse and a justification (at p. 60, above). An excuse is a defense, such as insanity, provocation, or diminished capacity, that releases one from responsibility but does not make one's action praiseworthy. If one kills from insanity, one is not guilty of murder, but we still deplore the killing. A sane person helping the insane defendant in the killing would be guilty of murder and deserve punishment. A passer-by who stopped the killing would deserve our praise.

By contrast, a justification is a defense, such as self-defense, that releases one from responsibility in such a way as to make one's action praiseworthy. If the defendant received help, the accomplice would also be acquitted. A passer-by who prevented the killing would incur our censure and might even be guilty of a crime. As our law students learn to repeat in their sleep, it is a crime to assist an excused violation of law, and no crime to prevent one, but it is a crime to prevent a justified violation of law, and no crime to assist one.

As Tally has shown, necessity is a justification, not an excuse (at p. 60, above). If it is really possible to kill from necessity, then the killers (as Springham correctly but inconsistently noted at p. 54, above) deserve our praise and respect. Moreover, anyone who might have hindered the killers would deserve our censure and might even be guilty of a crime. But here we see the limit on Tally's argument: necessity does not apply to this case, or indeed to any killing of a person not in self-defense. If the spelunkers killed Whetmore from necessity, *then it would have been wrong for Whetmore to defend himself.* But this is absurd, as Tatting seemed to be arguing in *Spelunkers I* (at p. 16, above). Therefore, the spelunkers are not entitled to a necessity defense.

This, incidentally, is one sufficient reason why Justice Hellen is wrong to say (at p. 68, above) that general community notions of justice support this use of the necessity defense. Community notions of justice would undoubtedly allow Whetmore to defend himself.

IV

The case against a general necessity defense for killing does not require the radical nonsense of Justice Trumpet. I do not believe that a Supreme Court Justice in this or any other nation has ever argued that the self-defense exception to the prohibition of murder ought to be overturned. If Justice Trumpet did not already exist, then a parody that invented him would be dismissed as unbelievable. Someone should tell him that Socrates and Jesus were not legislators of Newgarth. Someone should tell him that there are many moral principles that, for good reason, are not incorporated into our criminal law, such as the prohibitions of covetousness, lust, and gluttony. Just as not every vice is or ought to be a crime, not every virtue ought to be a legal obligation. Some virtues are supererogatory, such as volunteering to die so that others may live. No one has a legal duty to die. The law can only demand that we abstain from a certain critical set of harmful behaviors, not that we be saintly. Justice Trumpet is guilty of wishful thinking in the way peculiar to moral fanatics. If he is quite sure that the law *ought* to be a certain way, then he is quite sure that it already *is* that way, and that those who disagree with him are *ipso facto* mistaken. Justice Trumpet is so determined to carry his dogma to the end that he concludes that all Newgarth judges, in all our courts, for tens of centuries, have been mistaken on the legal status of self-defense. The very claim proves that he is talking about natural law, divine morality, or moral logic, but not the human-made laws of our Commonwealth, which alone he has authority to enforce. Another form of the same delusion, common in our academic journals, is to believe that because law ought to be consistent, then it is consistent. Like the professors who write such articles, Justice Trumpet lectures on a principle that he was taught as a child as if he were teaching children. But actual law is no more ideal law (to quote Jeremy Bentham) than hunger is bread. Bentham's analogy is particularly apt here, for if the spelunkers had the same gift of wishful thinking that Justice Trumpet has, they would never have grown hungry.

V

Would holding the spelunkers guilty deter future spelunkers who found themselves in a similar situation? Justice Hellen argued that it would not (at p. 69, above). Here is one reason why she is wrong. We may fairly presume that these spelunkers were friends who cared for one another, not random partners on an expedition. Whetmore was the friend of the surviving spelunkers, and they were his friends. These spelunkers were not at all hardened criminals to whom cold-blooded killing comes easily. The prospect of killing their friend in cold blood must have been infinitely horrible. Yet something overcame their extreme reluctance. What was it? They tell us it was their strong desire to live and their perception that this horrible act was necessary for them to live. I grant their claim. But granting it entails that their only reason for killing their friend would have been neutralized if they had known with good certainty that the killing would lead to their own execution. For then they would know that to kill their friend would not save their lives, but seal their deaths. I propose that it does not take much to deter friends from killing and eating friends.

I do not claim that the deterrent effect of a guilty verdict is, in itself, a good reason to render a guilty verdict. But because I find the defendant guilty on independent grounds, I think it important to clarify that punishing him would serve a more useful end than mere retribution.

Now what if this analysis is incorrect and executing these spelunkers will have no deterrent effect whatsoever? If believing deterrence to be unlikely is even one factor that leads us to acquit the present defendant, then we will face a paradox. For the next time spelunkers find themselves similarly situated, the legal precedent that will influence their conduct (under our hypothesis) will be our acquittal, and that fact can only make killings of this kind *more* likely. In this sense, belief that punishing one defendant will deter others is like the belief that we can leap across a three-meter chasm. Casting our vote that it is so will not make it so. But casting our vote that it is not so, will make it not so. (If law displays these self-fulfilling effects, we have yet another reason to see it as an enterprise of human choices full of risk and passion, not just as a system of rules.)

VI

Having found the defendant guilty of murder, I append a final reflection on Burnham's insistence that we not bend to the feelings of sympathy that he feared lay behind the various arguments for acquittal. First, he draws a false dichotomy between feelings and reasons, and undermines his own consistency in elaborating it, as we will show below. Second, sympathy is not monolithic. We can be sympathetic to starving spelunkers, but we can also be sympathetic to the murder defendants past and future who share important mitigating factors with these spelunkers but who are condemned to death just the same.

To take the second first: We have much data on how our murder statute, while neutral on its face, has been applied disproportionately against racial minorities and the poor, even after correcting for the increased rate of crime in these groups. This discriminatory impact is compatible with the statute's constitutionality, but it raises legitimate constitutional suspicions and forces us to interpret the statute's words in light of this social context, and with an eye toward correcting the imbalance in its historical application. To read the statute abstractly or outside the real social and historical setting in which it operates will only tempt us to disregard the equal protection of the laws and perpetuate the injustice.

This is a privileged defendant; spelunking is a sport of the affluent. His comrades were equally privileged; their execution was a small exception against the background of acquitting the privileged and convicting the underprivileged. It is important for us, then, to hold firm to the principle that the murder statute applies to defendants of this class. Murder defendants who offer defenses of necessity, duress, and diminished capacity based on the exigencies of poverty and disadvantage uniformly lose in our courts. To recognize a necessity defense for this affluent spelunker would only aggravate the discriminatory impact of the law and show this Court's indifference to its burdens.

Obviously this argument would be monstrous in the absence of sound, independent legal reasons to deny the defendant a necessity defense and convict him of murder. But conversely, it would be monstrous to ignore this argument when buttressed by sound, independent legal reasons for the defendant's guilt.

Now, as to the first: Is there really a qualitative difference, and no overlap, between our feelings of sympathy for the defendant and our legal reasoning about his guilt or innocence? Does Burnham believe that his reasoning about law has an immaculate conception? He talks at length, even with some feeling, about the diversity and disagreement in our society, what he calls its "pluralism" (at p. 43, above). He even insists that these plural views are of equal validity in the eyes of the law. But does he not see that this conclusion is at odds with his belief in a Legal Reason that is beyond faction, beyond ideology, beyond feeling, beyond nature and history? He tells us in effect that there is never one right answer in the eyes of the law, and then he tells us what the one right answer is in this case. He acknowledges that people have different backgrounds and experiences, and that these shape different legal and political philosophies; but then he hopes to transcend this swamp of difference with his "meta-level" pronouncements about what the law requires. Does he not see that what the law requires is itself a question on which different people legitimately have different views? We reason about statutes and cases, but we learn to reason from teachers and examples that are fully situated in history and embody interests and background assumptions that we will never fully disclose to ourselves and disentangle. We inflect this learning with our understanding of what is at stake, our feeling that it matters, and our passion to do what is right.

No one reasons outside a context, and the context always influences the purpose and content of one's reasoning. The context includes the community that shaped one's thinking, the history that shaped the community, the feelings of the body that struggle for words, the language that channels the words available to us, the problem that demands solution, and the interests that constrain acceptable solutions. To adapt one of Pascal's remarks about reason in religion: law without reason would be absurd and abhorrent; law limited to reason would be unjust and abhorrent. Reason without feeling can build death camps; feeling without reason cannot find effective means to resist. In healthy and constructive thought, even in law, even in mathematics, reason and feeling collaborate; they are no more separable than melody and tempo. To separate them is to oversimplify life, which we usually do for some definite purpose or other. This simplification is not motivated by understanding and rigor, but by fundamentalism and fear of complexity. Law is easier if it is just rules of conduct related by rules of inference; but unfortunately, law is as nuanced as life.

Reason does not come from God and feeling from DNA; both are artifacts of culture, like law itself. Law cannot rise above culture and the full human context, and always becomes distorted and one-sided when it tries. Of course the defendant is to be convicted or acquitted by the law, and the law alone. But it does not follow that he is to be convicted or acquitted by *reason* alone, as if that were a requirement of law – or even possible. Our sympathy for the defendant, or lack of it, is one of the motive forces of legal reasoning; we cannot abstract from it and we would dehumanize ourselves and our law if we tried.

I vote to uphold the conviction.

OPINION OF JUSTICE FRANK

I would have joined the lottery. If I were a winner, then I would have helped to kill the loser and I would have eaten my share of him. I cannot condemn, let alone execute, any man for doing what I would have done. When a judge finds himself punishing people no worse than himself, he should step down. When the only judges to be found who would punish certain defendants are those willing to punish those no worse than themselves, then the law is shamefully exposed. This is my reason for voting to acquit.

I am not sure that I can distinguish what I would have done from what I hope I would have done. I hope I would have waited until the very last moment before accepting the necessity to kill anybody. But then I hope I would have urged that we use a lottery to select the victim and share the risk equally. I hope I would have had the courage to exert my share of energy, and implicate myself fully, in the act of killing. Finally, I hope I would still have had an appetite to save my life. Perhaps I would have withered from weakness; I will not pretend to be sure. But if I cannot condemn men for doing what I would have done, then *a fortiori* I cannot condemn them for doing what I hope I would have done.

I hear all my brothers and sisters ask: Where are my authorities? Where are my arguments? I hear them object: I offer no legal argument, but only speak about what I would have done myself and the scruple that prevents me from condemning men no worse than myself.

I reply that surely I could dress up my objection in legal garb, but another scruple prevents me from taking such an evasion. The length of Springham's opinion shows that dressing up my objection in legal garb is not a simple matter. Essentially, I endorse Springham's position, but I do not join his opinion. It is important to me not to use legal garb to cover my stake-taking passion in this case. Look at the controversy between Justices Hellen and Goad. Hellen is essentially saying that she would have killed Whetmore, and Goad is saying that she would not. But they dress up these autobiographical reports in the legal language of deterrence. We do not know whether punishing these spelunkers will deter other unfortunate people similarly situated in the future, but we now know that it would deter Goad and would not deter Hellen – or so they say.

We can speculate on whether the executions of four, maybe five, spelunkers would deter us. I am not criticizing this exercise of imagination. On the contrary, I think the exercise of imagining what we ourselves would do in a hypothetical situation is an essential part of the ethical life, and underlies such virtues as kindness, friendship, sympathy, compassion, toleration, and even-handedness. My point is that this exercise of imagination, or this autobiographical report, is as relevant to a judge's legitimate task when it is avowed as it is when it is disguised as a discussion of deterrence.

In this sense, the present case is not at all "hard." I know what I hope I would have done in that cave, and I know that I cannot in conscience punish men who did what I hope to have done. But in another sense, the hardness of this case is so acute and uncommon that this is the first in my career as a judge in which I have felt impelled to throw off the mask of judicial objectivity and rest on naked autobiography.

I vote to acquit.

OPINION OF JUSTICE RECKON

I

Justice Trumpet correctly concluded that necessity is irrelevant to this case, and the spelunkers guilty; but he came to this conclusion for the wrong reasons. He argued that a necessity defense for murder is incompatible with the sanctity of life; but even if true, this argument belongs in a pulpit, not a court of law. The true reason why necessity is irrelevant to this case is that, even if the present killing was necessary in the strongest sense, it would still be rational for Newgarth to punish those who did the deed.

Justice Springham correctly described one legal function of necessity: it negates *mens rea* or criminal intent. That makes it an excuse. For my purposes here, it may also be a justification, signifying that the defendant chose the lesser evil. Necessity can be both. Debating which one it is, as if it could be only one, is futile and beside the point.

Insofar as it negates criminal intent, we may call necessity a "mental defense" or "volitional defense." When present, it establishes that the defendant lacked the state of mind that the legislature wished to punish. But necessity is also an affirmative defense. Hence, when pleading necessity, the defendant concedes that he committed the act that the legislature wished to prohibit.

Now if a defendant committed a prohibited act, but without the punishable state of mind, then should we convict or acquit? The conventional answer to this question is that we should acquit. But the conventional answer is deeply flawed, as judged by moral, legal, and political criteria with deep roots in our society. The present case gives us a welcome opportunity to overturn the conventional rule and live up to our common criteria more faithfully.

If we recognize no mental or volitional excuses, and punish all those who commit prohibited acts, then we accomplish three ends of significant social importance. First, we will remove dangerous people from our streets. Second, we will shorten trials and make punishment more swift and certain. Third, we will strongly deter others from committing the same acts. For study after study has shown that criminals are deterred much less by the severity of punishment than by the swiftness and certainty of punishment.

If the primary social function of the criminal law is to protect citizens from the special kinds of harm caused by criminals, then the continued recognition of the mental excuses aggravates the problem; it does not contribute to the solution. If "excuses have excuses," then they derive from secondary social policies outweighed by the policy to protect the public from criminal wrongdoing.

Our reluctance to punish those who lack the requisite state of mind is based on the theory that threats of punishment will not deter children, the insane, the intoxicated, or those moved to act by ignorance, mistake, duress, or necessity. That is true but irrelevant. To punish them anyway, for their proved harmful acts, would protect us from them in the future and deter others. If citizens knew that no excuses would be heard in criminal trials, and that guilt would turn solely on the performance of the prohibited act, then we may be quite sure that many more people than presently would take pains to err on the side of compliance with the law.

Conversely, if citizens knew that certain mental or volitional excuses would be available to them, then not only would many of them be less frightened of criminal penalties, but many who did not deserve to be excused would win acquittals through cunning and sophistical trial tactics. Most of the mental or volitional excuses are states of mind that even experts cannot define with precision or prove to be present – or absent – with solid evidence. So to make these excuses available will call into being an entire industry of jury-consulting, poll-taking, expert-witnessing, syndrome-documenting, charge-caviling, blame-shifting, responsibility-denying, counter-indicting defense lawyering to take advantage of these excuses, much as we have seen in this Commonwealth in recent years.

If we are inclined toward the doctrine that abolishes mental or volitional excuses, then we need not say that punishing children or the insane is in itself a good thing. We need only say that the benefits of doing so outweigh the costs. It may be regrettable, like all punishment, but nevertheless justified. When a defendant commits a prohibited act but can prove insanity or necessity, then we clearly face a conflict of values, and we need not pretend that the case is easy. The doctrine that abolishes excuses does not deny the reality of this conflict; it merely solves it in one way rather than the other. Most citizens will agree, however, that reducing crime is a weightier social policy than releasing wrongdoers from punishment simply because they lack the vague and indefinite state of mind we call criminal intent.

Similarly, to support this doctrine we need not say that deterrence is the only, or even the chief, rationale for punishment. All we need say is that it is one genuine rationale for punishment. That is enough to start the deterrence pan of the scale moving downward under the weight of the arguments adduced here and elsewhere for this doctrine. Other rationales for punishment, which may intrinsically recognize excuses and justifications, must sit in the other pan and prove their weight in a detailed comparison of social advantage.

This argument applies just as strongly to justifications as to excuses. Whether a defendant chose the lesser evil is just as subject to controversy, and therefore just as inviting to sophistry, hair-splitting, and expert disagreement, and therefore just as costly and arbitrary to resolve, as whether the defendant had or lacked a loosely described state of mind.

Crime is terribly expensive, in lost and damaged property, in prevention and detection technology, in insurance premiums, in police salaries, in attorneys' fees, in prison and court costs, in trauma, in lost opportunities, and in the many ways that life is cramped and compromised by the need to live with the measures and institutions we have so dearly purchased. To make a significant reduction in crime would be as large a contribution to social wealth and happiness as making a significant reduction in disease or war. Some criminals would be less happy, of course, but even they would choose to reduce crime and live in the vastly improved society that would result if they had to make the choice as disinterested framers of a constitution, without regard for the misfortunes, pressures, and interests that in the present order of things might lead them to a life of crime. Eliminating the mental and volitional excuses, then, compared to retaining them, would be morally more beneficial, materially more conducive to production and the efficient allocation of resources, and politically more acceptable (grounded in a wider base of consent). A fault system might meet these criteria best in the civil law, but a no-fault system meets these criteria best on the criminal side.

The doctrine I am proposing would make strict liability for criminal acts the norm rather than the exception. But I find that the phrase "strict liability" prejudices the conventional legal mind without illuminating it. So I would prefer to see the case for this doctrine argued on the compelling ground of crime reduction and maximizing social satisfaction, without the use of inflammatory labels.

II

But this Court has again refused to endorse the proposal to abolish excuses and justifications for criminal behavior. For the time being, then, we must conclude that necessity, if proved, would suffice to acquit the defendant. Consequently I join the opinions of Justices Burnham and Goad that the defendant did not kill from necessity.

III

Several of my colleagues wonder whether punishing the defendant will "serve the purpose" of the murder statute or even the purpose of punishment. Justice Burnham does not answer this question, and Justice Goad, although correct in her analysis, does not say enough about deterrence to satisfy, e.g., Justice Frank. I have a few words to say on the subject of deterrence, although not nearly enough, I am sure, to persuade one like Frank, who has so far abdicated his reason that he is willing to admit it.

93

The most rational basis for punishment is to prevent criminals from taking advantage of non-criminals. Good citizens who obey the law are peaceable and non-violent. This is both a cause and effect of their willingness to obey the law, for the law prohibits violence. But the non-violence of a large sector of society creates opportunities for less scrupulous citizens. Non-violent people make easy targets. In this sense, good law and good people create a bed of temptation and opportunity in which crime grows. There is no natural deterrent to this kind of crime. The reason is simply that this kind of crime is rational; criminals may gain more than they lose by engaging in it. (Without a special deterrent, we could not avoid *this* sort of crime even if everyone were saintly, unless saints were irrational; but in any case, making everyone saintly is not a "natural" solution to the problem.) The only deterrent is the unnatural, human contrivance of punishment.

It is true but paradoxical to say that good people *incite* crime. But it is not at all paradoxical to draw the consequence, which is that only punishment can give the criminal a reason to think twice. But for punishment, crime would pay, and cost–benefit calculators would be attracted to it.

Impulsive actors cannot be deterred by any provision of law. But rational actors can be deterred by any penalty whose gravity, discounted by its probability, exceeds the gain expected from a crime. Moreover, almost miraculously, punishment tends to convert impulsive actors into rational actors who can then be deterred. (This conversion, however, is slow and haphazard because the impulsive are not rational enough to be converted quickly by rational considerations; the conversion shows over a large population and a long time, not for individuals.)

People who obey the law give each other the great gift of peace and freedom, the highest goods of civic life. At the same time, they give criminals the gift of easy pickings – as well as the gift of peace and freedom. If this double gain were the whole story, then it would induce all rational actors to become criminals, at least initially. But rational actors would have to reflect that, if they all turned to crime, then no one would any longer have either the gift of peace and freedom or the gift of easy pickings.

This is a non-technical way of saying that the question whether to obey the criminal law is a *prisoner's dilemma*. The term comes from the situation of two prisoners in police custody who have committed a crime together. Suppose that the police have only enough evidence to charge them with a lesser crime unless one of them can be made to give state's evidence. If interrogated separately, each must decide whether to betray the other in order save himself, or whether to tell an exculpatory lie and hope that his partner does the same. If each supports each other by lying to the police (if they *cooperate*, as scholars on this subject like to say), then they are both charged only with a lesser crime and serve light sentences, say, of one year. If they betray each other (if they both *defect*), then each accuses the other of a serious crime and is willing to testify, so they are both convicted; say they each get three years in prison. If one betrays the other, but not *vice versa*, then the betrayer wins immunity from prosecution and is released, while the hapless partner is caught lying and given the full sentence for the serious crime, say, five years. The table or *payoff matrix* embodying the assumptions we just made appears in Figure 1.

Obviously the particular numbers need not be those chosen for this illustration; but their relative sizes must be as illustrated here. Defectors who betray cooperators must be better off than mutual cooperators, who must be better off than mutual defectors, who must be better off than betrayed cooperators. The betrayed cooperator is the kind of person we are most concerned about; let us give such people the shorter name, *chumps*.

Obeying the criminal law is a prisoner's dilemma because the highest gain goes to criminals who take advantage of, or betray, law-abiding citizens; they enjoy both their booty and the peace and freedom created by the obedient. The next highest gain goes to the obedient, or cooperators, who give each other peace and freedom but no criminal booty. Next are criminals who victimize each other; they have the booty they take, but not the booty taken from them, and of course they lack the peace and freedom created by the obedient. At the bottom

		Prisoner B	
		Cooperates	Defects
Prisoner A	Cooperates	A gets 1 year B gets 1 year	A gets 5 years B gets 0 years
	Defects	A gets 0 years B gets 5 years	A gets 3 years B gets 3 years

Figure 1

95

are the chumps, law-abiding citizens who are victims of crime without the fruits of crime to compensate them.

Now the reason to bring the technicalities of the prisoner's dilemma into our discussion is that it is the most succinct and elegant way to establish (1) that it is rational to cooperate only with other cooperators, (2) that it is rational to defect against defectors, (3) that law-abiding citizens can be chumps, and (4) that when defection is rational, there is no deterrent to it except punishment of an offsetting magnitude.

If we accept the argument that the defendant acted from necessity, must we acquit him? Or might we still have a good reason to punish him? If this was the sort of crime in which law-abiding cooperators were made chumps by rational defectors, then punishment is justified in order to make defection more costly than cooperation and to deter future rational defectors who find themselves in the same situation.

Now we can assume that the spelunkers are rational cost–benefit calculators. One piece of evidence is their lengthy discussion of the mathematics of the lottery. Another is the tendency of even unreflective people to seek their own advantage and to find it. If the spelunkers were rational criminals, therefore, the question becomes whether they were the sort who need punishment, that is, the sort to take advantage of the scruples of the law-abiding. Is that the case here?

The answer is *yes*. The spelunkers showed that they were willing to kill a person who was unwilling to kill a person. They were willing to defect against a cooperator. They were willing to make a chump out of a law-abiding citizen. When Whetmore backed out of the lottery and expressed his desire to wait a week, he was saying in effect that he wished to obey the law against murder. This made the others safe from Whetmore for at least a week. But how did they use their safety and liberty? They took advantage of it at the expense of the man who made it possible, and killed him.

This is a classic case of defectors exploiting a chump. Hence it is the classic case in which punishment is justified to increase the loss naturally arising from defection until it always surpasses the price of cooperation, even for chumps. Then and only then can we expect a rational actor to choose cooperation. Only punishment can make rational actors in this situation obey the law.

Citizens deciding whether to obey the law feel the pressures we have just described, just as partners in crime, separately interrogated, feel the pressures of the prisoner's dilemma. But of course we need not claim that citizens and prisoners consciously work out the details of their payoff matrix. We claim only that history shows that laws that would inspire compliance from hypothetical, rational, cost–benefit calculators tend over time to inspire compliance from real human beings with the full panoply of desires, interests, evasions, delusions, and temptations that prevents them thinking rationally.

IV

Before closing I would like to reply to Justice Hellen's attempt to strengthen her argument for the necessity defense by overturning *Commonwealth and Valjean* (at p. 67, above). She declares that *Valjean* was wrongly decided because it reflects the "class bias" of the Court and system of criminal justice. She wishes to replace it with a legal doctrine recognizing the state's responsibility to ameliorate poverty when private charities are insufficient to the task, and exculpating the "desperate poor" who commit crimes because the state has not met its obligations.

Does she object to *Valjean* because it was based on ideology rather than law? Or does she object because it was based on bad ideology rather than good ideology? Her notion that the state should ameliorate poverty and condone crime caused by poverty it did not ameliorate is, let us say delicately, not written into our constitution. It is not law but a political proposal. It is a political ideology. Consequently, if she objects to *Valjean* because it was ideological, then she must apply the same objection to her own alternative. If she objects to *Valjean* because it was bad ideology, then she confesses that her alternative is merely another ideology. Either way she undercuts her proposal.

All this is most ironic, for she is aware of Justice Burnham's objections to judicial legislation and judicial appeals to justice beyond law, and she has tried to answer his objections explicitly. But her answer to Burnham is limited to the claim that judges should implement the better political ideology when they can, for this will tend to nudge the law closer to ideal justice. This is to say that judges should behave like legislators, which it was precisely Burnham's purpose to deny. Hellen has not only begged the question of the limited and proper role of judges in our legal structure; she has tried to set a precedent that would work against her own vision of justice. For if her favored ideology were ever embodied in legislation, she would want the judiciary to apply it with loyalty, consistency, and restraint, not to subvert, second-guess, or supplant it. For the same reason, she has tried to set a precedent that would work against every person's hope that justice can be embodied in legislation.

To citizens of Justice Hellen's persuasion, it would not matter that her position violates the judicial oath and the spirit of democracy if it took a real step toward a more just system of law. Unfortunately, while I believe that her position fails to take such a step, I cannot show that here without imitating her in using a judicial opinion to air personal political views. This I will not do. But I can make the logical observation that her argument is a perfect specimen of special pleading. She shows that there are reasons to oppose the *Valjean* rule and to favor an alternative, as if this were not true of every legal doctrine ever enunciated by a human being. Does she ever consider the reasons to favor the *Valjean* rule or to oppose her alternative? Not once. Does she ever compare welfare to markets, or regulation to efficiency, as means of showing compassion and improving the lives of the poor? Not once. She has offered a preference but not an argument; she is a partisan but not an inquirer; despite her talk of diversity and pluralism, she does not take disagreement seriously. History teaches us that demagoguery of this kind is very unlikely to have social good on its side. If it were, then the refined experience of generations would have taught us to let isolated geniuses, like herself, rather than the refined experience of generations, design our political institutions.

V

Finally, I must reply to Justice Frank's peculiar argument that he cannot punish men for doing what he would have done himself in the same circumstances. Judges would have to be angels for this view to be compatible with the effective administration of justice. But, on the contrary, the first premise of law is that judges are human; that single fact explains virtually everything that is difficult, interesting, and important about law. Judges need not possess the virtues that criminals lack. They need only the virtue of knowing the law with clarity and precision, and the virtue of applying it with courage and consistency. If they possess these virtues, then their other vices, no matter how numerous or anti-social, will not interfere with their judging. I can easily imagine punishing a defendant for a vice I share. Suppose I smoke hemp-weed on weekends. I might regret this vice in myself and wish to suppress it in my own case. Or I may join the legislature in wishing to use the criminal law to suppress it in myself and others. I may even be proud of my proclivities, and zealously advocate a change in the laws, but nevertheless find my duty as a judge to lie in deference to the decisions of the legislature when it acts within its constitutional authority. For any of these reasons I might find a defendant guilty of violating our laws against the illicit use of controlled substances. This would not make me a *hypocrite*; it would make me a *good judge* who rose above his personal weaknesses to make the right decision on the law and facts of the case. Justice Frank's scruples would undermine all the reasons why we wish to have a government of laws and not men. In addition, he implies that in all the cases he has hitherto decided against criminal defendants, he has been in a position "to throw the first stone" – a claim that is as unnecessary as it is incredible.

I vote to uphold the conviction.

OPINION OF JUSTICE BOND

I

I must recuse myself from this case. When I was in private practice forty-five years ago, a partner in my firm argued unsuccessfully against the validity of a patent on a voltage meter used in the manufacture of the kind of batteries used in the radio by these spelunkers. A private investigator hired in part with my own funds confirms that batteries of the kind used by the spelunkers 50 years ago in their radio are routinely tested by the type of meter that was the subject of the patent controversy.

I would stop here and rest in silence, but more than one colleague has privately objected to my decision. They cite two grounds: first, that my connection to the patent litigation is too remote to warrant recusal, and second, that the batteries are not relevant to this case. I make no comment on the first ground. In our Commonwealth, judges may properly recuse themselves if in conscience they sense a real or apparent conflict of interest, even if other sensitive and informed people do not perceive it. The dictates of one man's conscience need not be shared by another; if it were otherwise, exemptions on grounds of conscience would not play the role in our law that they do.

On the second ground, however, I take the unusual step of explaining my reasons for recusal in some detail. In a case of this legal significance, followed with such close attention by the media, it is imperative to satisfy the parties and the public that I am not simply retreating from a difficult decision. I will limit these comments to those strictly necessary to show the relevancy of the batteries, so that I may avoid abusing my recusal by abstaining from the decision while offering an opinion at the same time. Unfortunately, however, the only way I know to explain the relevancy of the batteries is, while compelling, not brief.

II

My colleagues to a person are either sure that this killing was willful or sure that it was not willful. The warmth of this disagreement ought itself be a clue that

99

perhaps they are arguing about policy, not words. The term "willful" as applied to killings has a certain canonical, standard meaning. The core of the settled, standard meaning of the term refers to premeditation, intent, and voluntariness. But like every other adjective, such as "bald" or "tall," this term has an indeterminately large area of open texture where we cannot be sure that it does, or does not, properly apply. If a man's hairline has receded *just so far*, then we may call him "bald" or "not bald," at our pleasure, and not expect to hear anyone accuse us of misusing the language.

This case falls into the open texture of the term "willful." We may call this killing "willful" or "not willful" without misusing the term. The disagreement of learned judges, all native speakers of the language, establishes this immediately. (How plain can the plain meaning of the word be if Burnham and Goad think "willful" accurately describes this killing and Springham and Hellen do not?) But if the killing may be called "willful" or "not willful" with equal fidelity to the language, then this shows that we may no longer expect guidance in our decision from the word "willful."

But if we can expect no further guidance from the term "willful," then we can expect no guidance from the murder statute, for it convicts or acquits defendants solely through the concept of willfulness (when, as here, the taking of life is conceded). This is a case, then, in which our laws are uncharacteristically silent and unhelpful. This, then, is a perfect example of what is often called a *hard case*.

The only way to decide a hard case, where the relevant laws are vague or inconsistent or silent, is to find a standard external to the law. This is not a cynical or incendiary statement; it simply spells out the consequences of *hardness* in the present sense. Hard cases mean that the law is unhelpful, and the unhelpfulness of the law means that discretion is unavoidable, and discretion means that extra-legal standards must come into play. Resort to a standard external to the law, however, frightens colleagues of a certain political bent, for it opens the door to judicial legislation – a professional sin in most nations, but also a cause of past revolution, bloodshed, and misery in our own (see Justice Keen at p. 21, above).

But every hard case unavoidably opens this door. It is opened by the nature of things, for human legislators cannot capture the complexity of life in a net of rules. Even if legislators were not limited in their wisdom, they would be limited by their language. Legislators must express their rules in words, and words by their nature have settled meanings at the core and open texture at the periphery; and inevitably scenarios of life will arise that fall within the open texture. In this case the legislature failed to elaborate to a sufficiently fine level of detail the state of mind that the Commonwealth must prove before it convicts a defendant of murder. In other hard cases the insufficiency of articulation shows up at other points. But no conceivable finite addendum to our criminal code would suffice to cover without vagueness or open texture all the cases that actually arise in life.

My colleagues who fear judicial discretion, therefore, are like people who fear death. They fear the inevitable. The remedy is not to rail against the inevitable, a patently infantile response, but to quiet our fears, acknowledge the unavoidable role for discretion, and take pains to avoid abusing our discretion. Discretion does indeed contain the risk of judicial usurpation or abuse, but when exercised responsibly it need not rise to usurpation itself.

Justice Reckon's opinion neatly but inadvertently embodies my thesis. He fears judicial discretion, under the name of judicial legislation, and criticizes Justice Hellen for turning to it. But he proves that it is unavoidable by turning to it himself. For if Hellen's conclusions about poverty, social justice, and the responsibility of the state reflect her political ideology more than current law, then what shall we say of Reckon's proposal to abolish mental excuses, his preference for an exceptionless rule of strict liability, and even the priority he gives to the social goal of crime reduction?

For Burnham and Reckon, discretion is objectionable because it does not tie a judge's hands; on the contrary, it leaves judges free. But if Burnham and Reckon could have their way, and magically prevent judges from using any methods that left reasonable people free to disagree, then they would bring the administration of justice to a standstill, even if they could first replace all judges they regard as usurpers with judges more to their liking. In that regime, judges could only apply those laws that could be applied mechanically. But can anybody produce even one example of such a law? Judges could not apply any statute in which even one word required interpretation, and certainly could not adjudicate hard cases. Can this forced retirement be the "proper role" of judges they speak so much of? (See Burnham at p. 43, and Reckon at p. 97, above.)

Justice Springham argues that statutory interpretation, while not mechanical, is guided by standards, and that because the law already contains all the relevant standards, we need not resort to discretion or extra-legal norms in order to adjudicate even hard cases. This is to say that the law is never vague, silent, or inconsistent, but exceedingly vast and complex. But we are on the verge of quibbling about words. For if, on the one hand, the standards already in the law do *not* force a single decision mechanically, then the judge is free in a way that is well captured by the word "discretion." And if, on the other hand, the standards already in the law *do* force a decision, entirely without the aid of any extra-legal norms, then the process is really mechanical. The process may not be mechanical in practice because finite human judges lack the time, capacity, erudition, and resources to bring together, and hold together, all the factors from the vastness of law whose vector is the one correct outcome. But if so, then it is pointless to insist that the law already contains all the relevant standards, even if true; for finite human judges will be unable to ascertain them all and must still creatively develop applicable standards as if the law were vague, silent, or inconsistent. And this creative development of standards is, also, well captured by the word "discretion."

Although I have distinguished discretion from usurpation in order to console those who fear discretion, I believe it is more constructive to replace this fear with hope and hard work than to console it. I do not fear discretion at all, but welcome it. Discretion, and discretion alone, gives us a chance to find where justice lies in hard cases where (again, by definition) the law is vague, silent, or inconsistent. If a hard case is one that the legislature did not foresee or decide by its legislative language, then the hardness of the case means that judges will examine *for the first time* the issues the case raises, if anybody is to examine them. This makes discretion a precious opportunity to find justice, not a distressing risk of usurpation. Discretion allows us to face squarely the features that make a case difficult and to craft a resolution that fits those unique and difficult facts.

Someone might argue that this case was not entirely unforeseen by the legislature. In the wake of *Spelunkers I*, several proposals to amend the murder statute were raised in the legislature. In defeating them, the legislature was saying, in effect, that the present murder statute is adequate to deal with such unusual circumstances. By contrast, there was no basis to make this claim of legislative intent in *Spelunkers I*. While this position has a factual basis in legislative consciousness of the speluncean dilemma, it does not establish what the legislative intent is with the specificity required to make discretion unnecessary. Did the legislature intend that spelunkers in this situation be convicted of murder and be executed? We cannot say. It appears that a legislative majority was satisfied with the outcome of *Spelunkers I*. But the legislature's non-action could be due to the fact that the bloc wishing to amend the statute to insure guilty verdicts in cases of this kind was offset and neutralized by the bloc wishing to insure not-guilty verdicts. Moreover, the legislature knew that the language of the statute supported several reasonable theories of acquittal. Hence, even a clear majority satisfied with the outcome of *Spelunkers I* had a good reason to amend the statute to make its intention unmistakable in the future. Therefore, the legislature's non-amendment of the statute either raises doubt about the majority's position, or it throws us back to the uncertainty faced by our colleagues in *Spelunkers I*. Either way, we must ignore the complexity introduced by explicit non-amendment and deliberate as if the legislature had no intention for this case capable of guiding us.

If we try to minimize discretion, we end up relying on tenuous clues to the legislature's intent, belabored and over-interpreted, or rules intended for other branches of law, refracted by analogy, all to support our wishful thinking that the legislature did in fact have an intention for cases of this kind. But what we know about the present case, once we know that it is *hard*, is that the actual historical legislature never dreamed of this case, never examined the issues raised by this case, and never decided that the defendants in such cases were, or were not, to be punished as murderers. Therefore in hard cases legislative intent is non-existent and judicial examination of the facts and issues is the only possible path to justice.

This view of discretion has the virtue of answering an objection raised by Justice Keen. He believed that the statute requires us to convict the spelunkers, even if we have moral reservations about doing so. While he admitted to these moral reservations himself (at p. 24, above), he took a certain delight in finding the four defendants in *Spelunkers I* guilty. He even insisted that for judges to enforce the bad consequences of bad law has "a certain moral value by bringing home to the people their own responsibilities toward the law that is ultimately their creation, and by reminding them that there is no principle of personal grace that can relieve the mistakes of their representatives" (p. 24, above). In short, judges ought to lend their weight to the injustice of unjust legislation, for then the people will wake up and pressure the legislature to change the laws; this is better, he argued, than for the judges to change the laws themselves, as if these were the only alternatives.

The merit of discretion, however, is that it does not "change" the law so much as render its indeterminate fringes determinate. How the law applies to one kind of unforeseen case is then settled rather than still unsettled. This is a proper job for the judiciary, because it requires the application of general norms to particular cases. If the legislature did reform the law, it would leave new areas of open texture, requiring future exercises of judicial discretion. Keen tried to live up to his abstract principle by executing four defendants. That did indeed wake up the public, which called for a change of law, although without success. But surely in a Commonwealth civilized enough to settle its disputes in a court of law, we do not bring about legal change through human sacrifice.

III

Having found discretion unavoidable, and welcome, even if dangerous, I would then have undertaken a thorough investigation of the relevant moral and political principles that might inform the discretion of a good judge facing the present case. But to stick to those needed to show the relevancy of the radio batteries, I must detail only one small part of that investigation.

As more than one colleague has already found relevant to this case, the government of our Commonwealth was founded upon an explicit contract made by the survivors of the holocaust in the first period following the Great Spiral (see, e.g., pp. 12, 55, 81, above). But, as all contract philosophers observe, a government cannot originate in a social contract unless the original parties to that contract can withdraw from the nation or sovereign that previously held them, dissolving the bands of one government in order to forge new ones. But if our ancestors could withdraw from their former nation or sovereign, then modern Newgarthians may do likewise, for another principle of the contract view of law holds that the members of the founding generation shall not enjoy more liberty than their descendants.

This leads me to pick up a theme first aired by Justice Foster, that these spelunkers drew up for themselves, in their cave, "as it were, a new charter of government" (at p. 11, above). But I will be more direct and explicit: these spelunkers withdrew from the sovereignty of Newgarth and formed a new social contract inside the cave. A nation with a different history might scoff at our willingness to entertain such a theory. But to Newgarthians, the spectacle of men seceding from one nation to start another is not just a story of surpassing patriotic and mythopoeic power, but our most fundamental method of explaining to one another our obligation to obey the law through principles of consent and contract. For us, the obligation to obey is not eternal, deriving from reason or heaven. It turns on material events that arose at one point in our history, and might arise again. It is the rhythm of secession and establishment, renunciation and reunion, revolution and restoration, that explains law and nationhood for us, and that we see in microcosm in the present case.

In short, the spelunkers performed a peaceful revolution inside the cave. Now in deciding what to make of this fact, I must be cautious not to exceed my mandate and give a full opinion, for example, asserting that their peaceful revolution means that they were no longer subject to Newgarth's criminal law.

Before the men made the pact that I am calling a new social contract, they asked by radio for a legal ruling on their lottery plan (see p. 8, above). This indicates a willingness, even an eagerness, to follow Newgarthian law. But the silence of the Commonwealth in response to their query rings like a bell. In response to the silence of the state, the men turned off their radio and decided for themselves whether to adopt a new covenant with one another different from the covenant under which they had previously lived in Newgarth. Three days after they voluntarily turned off their radio, they killed Roger Whetmore (see p. 8, above). During those three days, I contend, the men solemnized their secession from the laws of Newgarth and their establishment of an alternative code under which to live and die.

I can imagine three objections to this account.

1. The men could not have intended to secede and form a new nation if they sought by radio to know and obey the laws of Newgarth.

This objection ignores the order of events. Yes, the men did initially seek to follow our laws. But when they received no help from us in doing so, they made a new and different decision, and they never again showed any curiosity about the requirements of our laws. Not only was their initial willingness reversed by later events, the events that led them to change their minds are manifestly the responsibility of the Commonwealth. Speaking broadly for the judges and officials of our state, *we* must accept responsibility for turning these men away from the doors of our law. Our clergy are equally guilty of failing to respond to the spelunkers' question (see p. 8, above). These two failures together left the spelunkers with no norms of church or state to guide their decisions, leaving them to rely on norms of their own devising – a new social contract.

2. The cost of the rescue was underwritten in part by a legislative grant of hundreds of thousands of frelars (see p. 7, above). This shows the Commonwealth taking responsibility for the men as if they still belonged to our society.

This objection is easily answered. At best it shows the attitude of the Commonwealth, not that of the men. The spelunkers might have made their revolution effective and complete without the consent of Newgarth; indeed,

Newgarth's consent would make revolution unnecessary. Second, the Commonwealth funds were apparently not expended until the private funds of the Speluncean Society were exhausted (see p. 7, above), showing our legislature anxious to avoid spending public moneys on the rescue until absolutely necessary. Third, the Commonwealth might well spend public moneys to rescue foreign citizens trapped inside a cave in our Central Plateau without conscripting the unlucky explorers to Newgarthian citizenship.

3. Finally, it might be objected that a Newgarthian judge on the scene might not have been able to condense our law into a sentence suitable for transmitting as the answer to the spelunkers' radio question. The spelunkers asked whether it would be advisable to throw dice in order to select a member of their party to kill and eat (at p. 8, above). My own view of open texture and discretion, as well as our several disagreements, suggest that Newgarthian law has no easy or obvious answer to the spelunkers' question. So a judge on the scene could not have answered their question without misleading them on the state of our law. Hence, the objection would go, we cannot blame Newgarth for its radio silence, which might have been more helpful and comforting than the disputatious disquisitions of nine Supreme Court justices.

This objection, while apparently strong, is beside the point and easily answered. First, no official of our government even tried to answer the spelunkers' question. We would have a very different case if an official had offered advice that the men followed but that the members of this Court found contrary to the actual dictates of our law, or if an official had given correct advice but the spelunkers had not followed it. In fact, however, no attempt was made. Second, the issue here is not whether it would have been easy to give an accurate answer to the men's question; it is whether the men had a reason to turn from Newgarthian law to laws of their own creation inside the cave. The state's radio silence, even if somehow justified or superior to the alternative, operated as just such a reason, throwing the men onto their own resources for coping with their situation.

Justice Tatting attempted to reduce Justice Foster's incipient version of this thesis to absurdity by asking (at p. 15, above), "If these men passed from the jurisdiction of our law . . . , at what moment did this occur? Was it when the entrance to the cave was blocked, or when the threat of starvation reached a certain undefined degree of intensity, or when the agreement for the throwing of the dice was made?" Foster might have had difficulty answering this question, for in fact he wavered inconsistently between the views that this killing occurred in the state of nature (at p. 11, above) and that it occurred under a new charter of government (at p. 11, above). But as refined here, this theory provides a most clear and compelling answer: the men passed from the jurisdiction of our law when they agreed to throw the dice, for that was the moment they adopted the pact that formed their new and superseding social contract. Similarly, Tatting facetiously wondered (at p. 15, above) whether the men were beyond our jurisdiction "because of the thickness of the rock that imprisoned them, or because they were hungry, or because they had set up a 'new charter of government' by which the usual rules of law were to be supplanted by a throw of the dice." Again the answer is clearly the third on Tatting's list. If Foster had lived up to the theory implicit in his phrase, "new charter of government," instead of confusing that sort of revolution with a return to a state of nature, or if Tatting had remembered the sufficiency of contract to establish a sovereign state, which all good Newgarthians learn in elementary school, then Tatting would not have thought his weak rhetorical questions amounted to a *reductio ad absurdum*.

When the starving men could not learn what Newgarth law required of them, they decided what to require of themselves. This reading of the case shifts the focus from the spelunkers' rights – for example, Springham's right of self-preservation or Trumpet's right of equality – to their responsibility to create a code of conduct and live loyally and consistently up to its terms. It is a needed corrective to the one-sided view that rights trump all other considerations, including responsibilities. It shows that rights and responsibilities are so intimately reciprocal that they can be established in the same act of consent, and reflected in the same throw of dice.

I need not reach many auxiliary questions here, such as whether their new code of conduct derived properly from the consent of those to be governed by it. If I were writing a full opinion, and not merely the fragment needed to show the relevancy of the batteries, I would fully explore the question whether Whetmore revoked his consent to the new pact; whether, if so, the spelunkers killed a citizen of Newgarth, thereby bringing their act within the jurisdiction of our laws; whether the very idea of revoking consent to a social contract evokes too much of the old individualism to be reconciled with the idea of a social contract itself (as if individuals constituted, rather than were constituted by, their societies); whether the spelunkers' acceptance of Newgarthian government services while in the cave – the subsidized portion of the rescue – establishes their tacit consent to Newgarthian laws; and whether the rationality that drove them toward their new state of law is Justice Reckon's pitifully shrunken and technical sort, Goad's sentimental hybrid, or the more full-bodied kind exercised by our ancestors when they formed the contract that underlies our Commonwealth.

IV

This argument turns critically on the change of mind that we infer must have taken place in the spelunkers after the Commonwealth met their radio question with silence. If there was no change of mind, then the spelunkers' initial willingness to know and obey Newgarthian law persisted and we would have little reason to suppose that the men turned from our law to form a new social contract.

Now we know that after the state refused to answer the spelunkers' question, the trapped men made no further radio broadcasts (Truepenny at p. 8, above).

Those in the rescue camp believed the radio batteries inside the cave must have gone dead, but this proved to be incorrect (p. 8, above). If the batteries had truly died, then we would not know what to infer from their radio silence; it could signify a change of mind or a failure of equipment. The men might have asserted at trial that they changed their minds inside the cave, and created a new state, but we could always suspect that they were fabricating for the sake of tactical advantage. But because we know the batteries still held their charge, we know that the spelunkers' radio silence was deliberate and voluntary. This fact supports our view that they turned their backs on Newgarthian law, after it turned its back on them, and drew up their own code of conduct to deal with their plight. It supports the view that the men effected a peaceful revolution.

This reading of the case puts uppermost our historic principle of deriving law from consent and contract, and yet depends essentially on the batteries in the spelunkers' radio. If the batteries had expired, our reading would be compatible with the known facts but entirely conjectural. Now I am careful not to say that this reading is the true one, and draw the consequence for the defendant's guilt or innocence. For I have waived my right to rule on the facts of the case. I conclude only that the capacity of these batteries to hold their charge is relevant to the outcome of the case, and hence that my entanglement with past litigation concerning equipment to test and monitor that capacity forces me to recuse myself.

I regretfully abstain.

The Supreme Court, being evenly divided, the conviction and sentence of the Court of General Instances is *affirmed*. It is ordered that the execution of the sentence shall occur at 6 a.m., Friday, April 3, 4350, at which time the Public Executioner is directed to proceed with all convenient dispatch to hang the defendant by the neck until he is dead.

INDEX